Simon Girty
The White Savage

Indian War Dance

Simon Girty
The White Savage

Thomas Boyd

COMMONWEALTH BOOK COMPANY
St. Martin, Ohio

Originally published in 1928.
This edition © 2022 by Commonwealth Book Company, Inc. All rights reserved. No part of this book may be reproduced in any form or by any means without the prior written consent of the publisher, excepting brief quotes used in reviews.
Printed in the United States of America.

TO
AGNES AND AIMÉE
AND ERIC

CONTENTS

CHAPTER	PAGE
I—"Then Girty's Name and Girty's Fame"	3
II—Excursions and Alarms	13
III—A Rough Neck's First Thirty Years	29
IV—Wherein the Scoundrel Saves a Hero from Roasting at the Stake	63
V—Simon Becomes Morose; His Scalp Causes Him Some Concern	91
VI—Those Damned Missionaries; and the Butchering and Burning of Their Hapless Brood	115
VII—Wherein Vengeance Carelessly Takes the Wrong Man	141
VIII—With One War Ended and None Other at Hand Simon Takes a Wife	169
IX—Wherein Two Generals Lose Their Armies	185
X—Simon Drives a Quill Through His Nostrils	207
XI—The Long Shadow of Mad Anthony Wayne	223
XII—The Last Ride from the Tavern	241

ILLUSTRATIONS

INDIAN WAR DANCE	*Frontispiece*
	FACING PAGE
TECUMSEH	40
SIMON KENTON	74
THEYANDENEGEA	126
SIR JOHN JOHNSON	178
BRIGADIER GENERAL ANTHONY WAYNE	224

"Then Girty's Name and Girty's Fame"

The White Savage

CHAPTER I

"*Then Girty's Name and Girty's Fame*"

AMERICAN pioneers who crossed over the Alleghanies and settled westward of Pittsburgh during the last quarter of the eighteenth century went into a wilderness where the forces of destruction flourished. Snakes, catamounts and bears—each had its way of killing; also floods, cyclones and diseases attacked the pioneers. Paint-streaked Indians fought these white interlopers moodily, self-defensive and revengeful, and for thirty years musket ball and speeding arrowhead crossed and recrossed over clearing and occasional plain. Cabins were burned, bark tents torn from their supporting poles, cornfields trampled and charred back into the earth. Scalps were ripped by Indian and white man alike. Mercy was a word not greatly honored by anyone.

It was a time of fury, those thirty years. Ambushes, marauds and murderous expeditions were carried on continuously. There were three major battles which rolled

THE WHITE SAVAGE

up their toll in hundreds, but when the last had been fought and the vast forests started crashing down the white men were there to stay and the Indians were herded into what was then the far northwest.

Those surviving white folk who settled western Pennsylvania, Kentucky and Ohio had tall tales to tell their youngsters. They had seen the harshest murders, the most providential escapes. They had been besieged not only by four strong tribes of Indians, but also by the British, who held Detroit and who worked hand in hand with the dark warriors to drive the frontiersmen back across the Ohio River.

Out of this warfare grew heroes and villains. The list of the former was a long one. It included names of Daniel Boone, Simon Kenton, George Rogers Clark, Mad Anthony Wayne, Colonel William Crawford, the Wetzel brothers and many others remembered in the west. The villains, quite naturally, were the enemies of the pioneers: among them were General Henry Hamilton, Lieutenant Governor of Canada; Captain Pipe, a war chief of the Delawares; Alexander McKee, a loyalist who had fled from Pittsburgh to take up service under Hamilton at Detroit; and Simon Girty.

Of all the men remembered from those years Simon Girty, who has been called the anomaly of western history, was perhaps the most widely and deeply hated.

"GIRTY'S NAME AND FAME"

Pioneer mothers in lonely cabins used to scare their children into obedience by threatening them with the appearance of the dreaded Girty. And afterward it was said of him that "no other country or age ever produced, perhaps, so brutal, depraved, and wicked a wretch." Another called him "a monster. No famished tiger ever sought the blood of a victim with more unrelenting rapacity than Girty sought the blood of a white man. He could laugh, in fiendish mockery, at the agonies of a captive, burning and writhing at the stake. He could witness unmoved the sacrifice of unoffending women and children. No scene of torture or of bloodshed was sufficiently horrible to excite compassion in his bosom." And in "The Romance of Western History" it is told that he was "a wretched miscreant" who "had fled from the abode of civilized men; he became a savage in manners and in principle, and spent his whole life in the perpetration of a demoniac vengeance against his countrymen." To an early midwest poet he was:

" 'The outlawed white man, by Ohio's flood,
Whose vengeance shamed the Indian's thirst for blood;
Whose hellish arts surpassed the red man far;
Whose hate enkindled many a border war,
Of which each aged grand-dame hath a tale,—
Of which man's bosom burns and childhood's cheeks grow pale.' "

[5]

THE WHITE SAVAGE

It was with such embellishments as these that Simon Girty's name was handed down from generation to generation of men who had come to live in the land of the Indian. He was looked on as a monster, and local historians treated him as one. They had him killed as they believed he ought to have been killed. In Wright's "History of Perry County, Pennsylvania" he was slain "in a desperate contest" by a colonel whose wife he was supposed to have stolen; in other works he was cut down and trampled to death by Kentucky horsemen at the Battle of the Thames.

As a matter of fact Girty survived his own death notice by several years. When he died it was from a prosaic illness. But up to that time his life had been made up of constant movement and adventure. From his youth he had seen heads split by tomahawks, had seen men roast inside a circle of burning faggots. His own father had been killed by a hatchet, his stepfather had been burned. In traveling over the Ohio and Kentucky wilderness, first as a scout and interpreter for the colonists, then for the United States and later as a renegade with the British, he built for himself a singular place in the history of his time.

Girty's life, particularly between 1774 and 1794, was so closely connected with the Ohio Indians during the years in which their country was being invaded by

"GIRTY'S NAME AND FAME"

American settlers that his story follows their successes and defeats like an historical narrative of them. He had been born on the border and had grown up amid its wildness. From childhood he had known Senecas, Delawares and Wyandots. Their manner of living in some ways suited him better than that of the frontiersmen. And when a combination of circumstances—in the third year of America's War of Independence—made him leave Fort Pitt and go to the British at Detroit he was unwittingly on his way to become a leader among the Indians.

His is the story of a backwoods roughneck who left his own people because of a slender grievance and for twenty years led raiding parties of Indian warriors through the Ohio wilderness to the white man's border, a dark, brawny man who fought as fiercely as a Shawanese chieftain. Over the Ohio into Pennsylvania, Virginia and Kentucky he rode at the head of marauding braves and left settlements smoking when he turned back. That the early pioneers had cause to hate him there is no doubt. Nor is there any doubt that they hysterically exaggerated his numerous cruelties.

But that was to be expected. For at lease twice in his career he stood in the light cast by his own former countrymen burning at the stake; and once he commanded a horde of Wyandot warriors who galloped into

THE WHITE SAVAGE

an American army which they were foremost in butchering. No name seemed black enough to discolor him.

However, this "wretched miscreant," than whom no country or age ever produced "a monster so brutal, depraved and wicked," had a disconcerting way of showing feelings that would have been praiseworthy even in men more humane than any that ever fought in a border war. Those frontiersmen were not noted for their gentleness. Neither was Simon Girty. Yet a number of times, and nearly always at the risk of offending the Indian chiefs and warriors, he pleaded or demanded that the lives of doomed white prisoners be spared. In the case of Simon Kenton, of whose captivity and death sentence there is a full account, Girty worked anxiously to save the Virginia scout—and he succeeded. That he often did successfully intercede for former countrymen of his who had been taken and condemned by the Indians is proved by records. There is the laconic deposition by William May in American State Papers (Indian Affairs), Volume one, page 242, in which he says he "was condemned to die; but saved by Simon Girty." And there is also the assertion of Jonathan Alder, who during his long years as a captive of the Indians met Girty often. Alder states that the renegade saved the lives of many white prisoners, sometimes at his own expense.

In short, Girty displayed too much humanity not to

[8]

"GIRTY'S NAME AND FAME"

have champions among the tender-hearted. And one of these, far from believing that Girty's "hellish arts surpassed the red man's far," came to his rescue with the following lines:

> "Oh, great-souled chief, so long maligned
> By bold calumniators;
> The world shall not be always blind,
> Nor all men be thy haters.
> If ever on the field of blood,
> Man's valor merits glory,
> Then Girty's name and Girty's fame
> Shall shine in song and story."

That optimistic prophecy, made many years ago, has not yet been fulfilled. Nor is this book an attempt to do so. Stubborn, bull-necked, proud of his strength, murderous yet merciful, Girty the traitor can't be whitewashed. But some credit should be given to the memory of a man who spent twenty years in the closest contact with the Shawanese, Miamis and Wyandots, rose to a position of trust among them and was, in fact, the only white person to sit as one of them in their tribal war councils. And while it would be fatal to defend him it may be interesting to see how far he can be explained.

Excursions and Alarms

CHAPTER II

Excursions and Alarms

S OMEHOW the American colonists always felt it queer that the Indians, who had inhabited this continent before them and who continued to live on in spite of them, should seriously object to giving up their land. Particularly was this surprise at aboriginal strangeness shown by the Pennsylvanians and Virginians.

Those two colonies were closest to the most thickly settled Indian country; it was over Pennsylvania or Virginia roads and rivers that western immigration had to pass, their boundaries that had to be expanded. Families voyaging down the Alleghany, up the Youghiogheny, down the Great Kanawha and the Little Kanawha westward pushed blindly into the Shawanese, Seneca, Wyandot and Delaware country with ax and musket and began to fell the forests and frighten off more game than they actually shot. And naturally the Indians resented it and used their tomahawks, their bows and arrows, and the gunpowder which the white men had sold them, to drive these irrepressible settlers back.

THE WHITE SAVAGE

That was the main reason why bloody terror stalked the length of the American frontier for half a century, why the bulk of the Indians south of Lake Erie and along the Ohio River joined the French against the English and fought with them until at the Treaty of Paris in 1763 the French admitted their defeat; the reason why these Indians later sided with the English after the colonies had rebelled and formed their own government; and also the reason why they continued to fight against the Americans for twelve years after Great Britain had formally acknowledged the United States of America. They were to fight, that is to say, until hope of success had completely gone. And altogether the showing they made was creditable rather than otherwise.

Had the French loved their own hearthfires less and ocean voyaging more the story of the American Indians during the eighteenth century would have been different from what it was. The men who explored the region of the Great Lakes and along the Mississippi down towards the Ohio were mostly French Jesuits and traders. They built churches and established trading posts beside the streams that moved throughout the wilderness, preparing the way for the emigrants from their own country. But these emigrants did not come; they preferred their few, well-cultivated gardens to all the timbered acres of the new world which they might have had for

[14]

EXCURSIONS AND ALARMS

the asking. And so the Jesuits and traders, while they failed to build an empire, were recompensed by few perplexing troubles which a hurried settlement of the land would have brought. They dealt only in religion and furs. The novelty of Christianity interested many of the tribes—not the Miamis, however—and gained many converts; the trade in skins pleased them all, for the Indians were given bright and useful things in return. And it was because of this that we find Indian warriors maintaining to the last that the French were the only white people whom they had ever voluntarily called their brothers.

The British, on the contrary, began life in the new world as colonizers. Self-righteous and determined, they had a lust for land and lordliness. Starting with the Plymouth colony and going down the coast this was true of nearly all the settlements except those controlled by Penn. In their harbors immigration flowered and from their villages men went out to penetrate the wilderness in search of permanent homes. In a long, disconnected chain they pushed westward, driving the Indians back, sometimes bargaining for what they took, but often wresting it by the superior force given them through ball and gunpowder in an arquebus or musket.

By the third quarter of the eighteenth century these men had become numerous enough to be able success-

[15]

THE WHITE SAVAGE

fully to defy the government under whose ægis they had settled. Englishmen, Scotchmen, Germans, Irishmen, Dutchmen and a few Frenchmen were willing to go to war rather than continue to pay the taxes on importations levied by the ministers of King George the Third. Englishmen of Virginia and Massachusetts took the lead in resisting the authority of Englishmen from England, and by the year the third quarter of the century ended the Thirteen Colonies were in a state of active rebellion.

That closed the coastline to all immigrants save those who wanted to come in as citizens of the United States of America. And thus Englishmen, per se, were shut out of the eastern seaboard and left with only Canada as a scene for future colonization. As the north slope of the St. Lawrence Valley was vast and as the tides from Europe drifted southward rather than towards Quebec, Canada remained thinly settled throughout the last half of the century. The British ruled it with their garrisons and their government, but the main business they carried on was the trade in furs.

So the English, in the minds of the Indians, came to take the place of the ousted French. They established forts, made trading posts beside the Great Lakes and along the main streams that drained the wilderness east of the Alleghanies and north of the Ohio River. There was no necessity for them to drive the Indians from their lands, for the area was enormous enough to swallow many times their number. They bought furs in exchange for rum and whisky, gunpowder, cloth, tools and shiny things; and both races were at that point content.

Had the contact between the Indians and the United States also been confined to trading, the western frontier would not have become such a ghastly nightmare of scalping, bloody tomahawks, devilish torture at the stake, indiscriminate murder and massacre. But that, of course, was impossible. The colonies were filled with people who had been born where land was precious and where only the richest owned great tracts. But they themselves had never been rich, in fact were unhappily poor, and the prospect of free acres in the wilderness of this new country tugged at them mightily. Always they were venturing out into the forests, making settlements on the ground from which the Indian had got his subsistence. And, Pennsylvania excepted, but only for a time at that, their colonial and state officers encouraged them. In 1770 Dinwiddie of Virginia had given away thousands and thousands of acres in the Indian country —land which was then being occupied by Shawanese, Mingo and Delaware tribes—and many of those who had received these grants were anxious to survey and make use of them. Their actions were those of a lordly, land-mad people and showed scant consideration for any rights the original possessors might have had. And the cultivated men of the time were no less grasping than the roughnecks of the border settlements. Quite typical, or even perhaps a little better than the average, was the attitude of George Washington, one time colonel in the Virginia militia, who had been awarded 10,000 acres and who had tremendously increased his holdings by buying more from others who wanted ready money.

Going out towards the Ohio country to investigate his wilderness estate, Washington was met by a Mingo chieftain who welcomed him to the country and assured him of his hope that the people of Virginia and the Indians would consider each other "as friends and brothers linked together in one chain." And Washington, his eyes open to the fact that the Mingoes would have to be driven away before his land could be settled, assured the chieftain "that all the injuries and affronts that had passed on either side were now totally forgotten, and that . . . nothing was more wished and desired by the people of Virginia than to live in the strictest friendship with them."

Yet he admits that these Indians had received "but little part of the consideration that was given for the lands eastward of the Ohio," that they "view the settlement of the [white] people on this river with an uneasy and jealous eye, and do not scruple to say that they must

EXCURSIONS AND ALARMS

be compensated for their right if the people settle thereon . . ."

"On the other hand," he goes on calmly, "the people from Virginia and elsewhere are exploring and marking all the lands that are valuable not only on Redstone and other waters of Monongahela but along down the Ohio as low as the Little Kanawha; and by next summer I suppose will get to the Great Kanawha, at least; how difficult it may be to contend with these people afterwards is easy to be judged of from every day's experience of lands actually settled. . . ."

Washingon rather thought that there might be trouble with the Indians, but that if there was it could be accounted for by the natural perversity of the aboriginal character and not by the fact that men like himself, men of the Ohio Land Company and also squatters, were pushing the Indians away from their villages. For while it was generally admitted that territory not fairly purchased by treaty still belonged to the Indians it was also taken for granted—by convenient mental sleight-of-hand—that the Indians had no right to it. And thus we find an American regular army major gravely taking the deposition of a man who told him that "from every observation he could make, and from the general talk of the Indians, he is led to believe that they are, in general, averse to giving up their lands" and, sur-

THE WHITE SAVAGE

prisingly enough, he is "certain it will be dangerous for the continental surveyors to go on with their business until some further treaty is made with the Shawanese, Mingoes and Cherokees, who appear to be most averse to this business."

The Indians, as both above quotations suggest, were a divided people. Except in the case of the Seneca-Iroquois confederacy each tribe had to be dealt with separately for a treaty to be of worth. Every tribe had its own dialect and customs, its own territory in which to live, hunt and cultivate the low-lying ground by the river banks. They were also capable of resentment, as most people are whose livelihood is threatened. Alarmed by the white men to the south and east, required and often forced to make treaties the natures of which they did not comprehend, they naturally had grievance against the colonies. When the colonies rebelled and set up their own government both English and Americans tried to bring them in as allies. But, as was to be expected, the English were the more successful.

It was not, however, until the second year of the revolution that the Ohio Indians appeared on behalf of either side. Up to that time they had fought the American borderers independently. But in the spring of 1777 Lord George Germain at Whitehall, London, passed upon a recommendation that had been made by General

EXCURSIONS AND ALARMS

Henry Hamilton, Lieutenant-Governor of Canada stationed at Detroit. Hamilton, out of the wilds of that far western trading post and garrison, had written to suggest that inasmuch as the Ohio forests were filled with Indian warriors it might be a stroke for the Crown if those braves were equipped with ball, powder and rations from the King's stores, guided by loyal Britishers and sent out to make "a diversion on the frontiers of Virginia and Pennsylvania." Receiving the letter through Sir Guy Carleton at Quebec, Hamilton soon afterward called a council of the tribes, the Shawanese, Senecas, Wyandots, Delawares, Ottawas, Chippewas and Pottawatomies.

Meanwhile the Americans were making an effort to enlist the support of the Indians, if for no other reason than to forestall their attendance at Hamilton's council in Detroit. This attempt to counteract the British organization of the tribes was begun from Pittsburgh where General Edward N. Hand was the commanding officer and George Morgan the agent of Indian affairs. Both men had positions of great responsibility, for Fort Pitt was the farthest and practically the only western stronghold on the colonial border; there was little between it and the British fort at Detroit except a few hundred miles of forest and prairie that were filled for the most part with displeased braves. It was therefore important that Morgan and Hand look well to their job, which was the conciliation of the Shawanese, Mingoes, Wyandots and Delawares, who occupied territory adjacent to the frontier.

Morgan went out to call the sachems and warriors to his council. Time passed. A few of them came, but the very paucity of their numbers showed that the majority preferred treating with Hamilton at Detroit. In the west the year 1777 drew to a close with settlers pushing towards the Ohio and into Kentucky and with the Indians retaliating with the gory tomahawk and scalping knife. In the east Washington was wintering his hungry, ragged soldiers at Valley Forge. At Detroit Lieutenant Governor Hamilton was making plans for a lively "diversion on the frontiers of Pennsylvania and Virginia."

At Fort Pitt the new year opened dismally. The fortification was old and crumbling, the town itself had not only patriots but also loyalists to England and lawless people who gave allegiance to nothing. Frequently somebody would be reported on the suspicion that he had been communicating with the British, would be locked up and later released because of lack of evidence. And sometimes the proof was there, but merely remained hidden. Up and down the border which Fort Pitt was supposed to guard small Indian parties fell upon lonely

EXCURSIONS AND ALARMS

cabins and left red tracks in the snow when they departed. Many pioneers thought desperately of the safe and pleasant homes they had exchanged for this life in the treacherous wilderness.

February came and General Hand, to check the blows of the Indians and to hearten the settlers, got together a force of five hundred men to attack a Delaware town on the Cuyahoga River. But by the time they had got as far north as the Mahoning the weather warmed; there were heavy rains which, with the thaws, swelled the streams until they were impassable. There, however, he had the misfortune to discover Indian tracks. At once his whole force went in pursuit of them. Following for some distance they came upon a solitary brave, some women and children! They killed the brave and one of the squaws, got hold of another squaw and took her captive. But the rest picked up their leathern petticoats and ran to safety.

It would have been less discomfiting for General Hand if his squaw prisoner had also escaped. For she told him that a number of Delaware warriors were nearby making salt, and at once he sent out a large detachment to attack them. The detachment was composed of the ordinary run of volunteers—men accustomed to play at "long shot" with their muskets in the crooked Pittsburgh streets and to nurse their offspring on whisky;

they went out to the salt lick and found four Indian women and a boy! But they seem to have had to whet their hatchets on somebody, and in lieu of the absent braves they murdered the child and three of the squaws. "One woman only was saved," are Hand's lugubrious words. His own loss was nearly as great, for he had a captain wounded and an enlisted man was drowned.

But Hand had barely got back from his expedition when another event made the Pittsburghers and the outlying settlers gloomier than they ever before had been; an incident that was greatly to increase their casualties during the revolution and that was to help keep the Ohio Indians steadfastly fighting the borderers for twenty years:

On the night of March 28, 1778, a strangely assorted group of seven men secretly left the neighborhood of Fort Pitt and struck out across the Ohio country on their way to Detroit. Two of them were Negroes, probably slaves. Another was a bland, canny man of property, a British loyalist who for some time had been Deputy Indian Agent at Fort Pitt for the Crown—Alexander McKee was his name. Another was Robert Surphlit, a cousin of McKee's. The fifth was "a man named Higgins." The sixth was Matthew Elliott, a short, snub-nosed Irishman who spoke several Indian dialects and knew the country well. And the seventh was Simon Girty, a burly, short-necked man of about thirty-six years whose jet black eyes looked out of a full, round face, a stocky, tireless man, a man full of petty pride, great personal courage, capable of ferocity and kindness, lasting hatred and lasting friendship.

No three men knew the Ohio Indians better than McKee, Elliott and Girty; no three men were better able to lead them against the border, and at no other time would their desertion have been so effective. Of these three it was Girty that was the most competent, that lived longest and most closely with the warriors. For he was among them from the spring of 1778 until 1795; the story of his life is more or less the story of the long fight of the Shawanese, Wyandots, Delawares and Miamis to hold the northwest, that is to say the Ohio country, for their own, and of their final effort which broke them up and left the Ohio River and the forest trails free to the pioneers who swarmed like locusts into the middle west, the northwest and the far west after cheap, productive land.

A Rough Neck's First Thirty Years

CHAPTER III

A Rough Neck's First Thirty Years

OLD SIMON GIRTY, an Irish immigrant who in the first half of the eighteenth century came to Pennsylvania and there engaged in packhorse driving for the Indian trade, named his second son after himself. Young Simon was born in 1741 at Chamber's Mill, five miles above the present site of Harrisburg, and very early in his life grew acquainted with the Indians and their ways. For Chamber's Mill was then on the verge of the Colonial frontier; it consisted of a huddle of rough log houses, a stockade named Fort Hunter, a mill and a tavern. To this settlement, which was hard-boiled even for those wild and ruthless days, came Senecas from the north, Shawanese from the southwest and Delawares and Wyandotes from the Ohio country to trade their furs for whisky, firearms and cloth.

But even that outpost of civilization was not far enough into the wilds for Old Simon. And when his second son was eight years old he removed his family across the Susquehanna to Sherman's Creek, where a score of Pennsylvanians had gone to make clearings and build cabins under the misapprehension that as this land belonged merely to the Indians it really belonged to the first white families that occupied it. The Girty family at that time was composed of Old Simon; his wife, Mary (Newton) Girty, an Englishwoman; Thomas, who was ten; young Simon, the next in line; James, who was six, and George, only a little more than a baby.

But these settlers on Sherman's Creek were mistaken about their right to the land. It belonged to the Indians by a treaty which at that time Pennsylvania took care not to break. And when the savages protested against this encroachment a number of Cumberland County deputy officers marched forth and set fire to the offending cabins. The pioneers were dispersed and the Girtys went back to Chamber's Mill.

In that settlement once more Old Simon took up trading with the Indians and drinking considerable potations of rum and whisky. Simon Junior was nine then. At best the family lived in a one-room log house with a kitchen built on at the back, and as the father entertained the Indian traders in the cabin the boy often saw white men and coppery men sprawling drunkenly on their stools, thumping each other on the back and falling at last quiescent on the bare floor.

For a year and a half this kind of life continued. A man named John Turner used to come there, also a warrior named The Fish. And with the elder Girty they would sit and drink and shout, until one December day, it was in 1751, more liquor flowed than could be handled. Suddenly The Fish became violent; lifting his tomahawk he brought it crashingly down on the skull of Old Simon. Whereupon John Turner, as a friend of the deceased and with an interested eye towards the widow, despatched The Fish among his ancient ancestors, and soon afterward became the legal stepfather to young Simon, Thomas, George and James.

If tradition is to be believed John Turner would have lived longer if he had let the death of the elder Girty go unavenged. For in the course of the next four years, while Simon was learning to bawl out roaring curses and take his liquor like a man, events were shaping for Turner's downfall. During that time occurred the wilderness war between the French and English, the purchase of a tract of land across the Susquehanna by the Penns; and at Chamber's Mill the stepfather discovered that he was unable to make a living for a wife and four ravenous boys.

He moved in the summer of 1755, taking the family near the site on Sherman's Creek where they had been before. There he built another cabin and made a late planting in the ground broken by his predecessor. But again the farming venture was cut short. For in July

THE WHITE SAVAGE

General Braddock discovered—too late, though, to make anything of the intelligence—that a host of scarlet coated men marching in close formation were of little account against a horde of Indians fighting under cover of trees and underbrush; and thus the border, after his defeat, was left with scant protection from Shawanese, Senecas, Delawares and the French. Within a year after Braddock went down, Neyon de Velliers, commanding twenty-three Frenchmen and about a hundred Indians, set out from Fort Duquesne, which afterward became Fort Pitt, then Fort Dunmore and finally the city of Pittsburgh, to attack the colonial settlements. They came to Fort Granville, on the Juniata, to which they laid siege. At word of their approach the frontiersmen about Sherman's Creek had come to Granville for protection. It was then nominally under command of Captain Edward Ward, but the day before de Villiers and his Indians surrounded the stockade Ward had marched his company of Pennsylvania provincials to gather the grain which the settlers had sown that fall. That left Granville with twenty-three men, John Turner, his wife, four stepsons and the recently born child which Mary Girty Turner carried at her breast.

De Villiers made several unsuccessful assaults, but in the midst of the last a group of Indians crept low along the banks of the Juniata and got near enough to shoot flaming arrows into the stockade. Soon the logs were blazing and the garrison asked for quarter. It was granted and John Turner let down the heavy bars to the stockade gates while the savages, headed by de Villiers, streamed through.

As prisoners the Girty family were marched away from the light of burning Granville. Taken westward to the Delaware town of Kittanning, on the nearer bank of the Alleghany, John Turner was tortured with red hot gun barrels, blazing faggots piled on his stomach, and a scalping knife slipped over his skull, while fifteen-year-old Simon, his brothers, and his mother holding John Turner Jr. in her arms, were forced to look on. After three hours a tomahawk ended the father's misery.

In the final division of prisoners, which occurred some weeks after the burning of Fort Granville, young Thomas escaped to Fort Pitt, Mrs. Girty, George and the infant were taken by the Delawares, while James was given to the Shawanese and Simon to the Senecas. These latter were the most advanced of all the Indian tribes in that part of the country; they had progressed so far as to have formed a confederacy with the Iroquois, Onondagas, Canandaiguas and Mohawks; their sachems, who were men of peace, were more powerful than their war chiefs and they had a fairly definite civil government. Thus Simon was particularly fortunate, for though he would have been treated equally well by almost any of the tribes he had the luck to begin his real acquaintance with the Indians in superior surroundings.

It was a general custom for prisoners either to be killed or adopted into some family which had lost a member in conflict. Simon's life was spared. Running a gauntlet made up of two rows of braves armed with sticks, he afterward went through the ceremony of naturalization which ended with three maidens taking him to a brook and there symbolically washing out his white blood and renewing his veins with the blood of the Secenas. From that moment he became a part of an Indian family and for about three years knew life as a young Seneca brave. He learned the language and customs of his foster people and was adept enough with the musket to be allowed to join the hunting parties by which his parents, grandparents, brothers, sisters, sisters' husbands and all the children were supplied with bear, venison and 'coon. He was treated as though he had been born of their flesh . . . an agreeable life for a youth who had no strong stirring towards the acquisition of private property, who would be content to share evenly with the old men, squaws, warriors and children in all things.

If Fort Duquesne (in 1758) had not fallen to General John Forbes and if that achievement had not been followed by a treaty with the Ohio Indians which required them in the following year to give up all their prisoners, Simon might very easily have lived on among the Senecas, taking an Indian wife who would have shared with him the labors of existence. He would have hunted with the braves, have gone on war parties when he chose, stayed in camp when he preferred and would have been well content, as were so many of the white borderers adopted by the Indians.

But the treaty made it necessary for him to go and he was curious to see his people. Some time in 1759 he said farewell to his Seneca relations and left them. They gave him of their supply of jerk and parched corn for his long journey southward to Fort Duquesne, which was now in the hands of the Pennsylvanians. After many days on the lonely trail he arrived; there he met his mother, his little half-brother, John Turner, his real brothers James, George and Thomas. All of them except Thomas had come in from the wilderness.

It was hard getting back into the stride of civilization, slow as it was at that place and time. Removed from an easy, communistic existence in which the feeling for private property had scarcely formed, Simon and his brothers had to find work in a society where personal ownership was a paramount urge. But he would, per-

THE WHITE SAVAGE

haps, have succeeded in returning to the more normal swing of things had his mother been more of a determined character with a more solid interest in family life. But apparently she hadn't, for after her return to Fort Duquesne she completely disappears from Simon's story. That left Thomas, at twenty, Simon, at eighteen, James, at sixteen, and young George to take care of themselves and hold together if they could.

But the very work which lay at hand separated them. Simon began to earn his living in the simplest and most unambitious way—becoming an interpreter for English and Pennsylvania traders who, now that the French were driven from the Ohio Valley, made Fort Pitt one of their chief headquarters. Strangely enough, though the Seneca tongue was best known to him, it was among the Delawares that he was principally employed. With the fur buyers he went repeatedly up into the northwest to the Muskingum and along that river towards the Tuscarawas, where he watched the exchange of warm, sleek skins for gunpowder, cloth and things that attract the eye. These sunburnt chiefs and warriors in their hunting shirts and jackets must have liked him; he must have shown himself to have been in some degree remarkable, for by the time he was twenty-three years old a chieftain of the Delawares, Katepakomen, had honored him by taking the name of Simon Girty.

However, his interest was not caught solely by the Indians. He voted at the first Bedford County election, which then included the whole of western Pennsylvania, and by the time he was thirty he had become "a man of talents" who possessed "great influence in the garrison (Fort Pitt) and with the Indians." Yet he acquired no property in or about the settlement of Pittsburgh. Like his brother James, he kept to his job of interpreter.

What then distinguished Simon among the frontiersmen was probably his understanding of the aboriginal mind and customs. He had a tendency towards their way of life. It is nowhere recorded that he made any effort to become a substantial citizen or that he shared at that time the almost universal itch for land which sent so many people, from George Washington down to the humblest squatter, journeying into the wilderness to stake out a claim. He had ambitions, it is true, but they were akin to those of the Indian and of the more romantic-minded white man: a desire for personal achievement and palpable recognition by his acquaintances. But as for Church and State, the bulwarks of civilized society, he had little use. Towards religion he was also, like his brother James, "a stranger . . . [without] any inclination to engage in such solemn matters contrary to the tenor of his life, having little or no fear of God before his eyes." But the Girtys were not unique in their atti-

THE WHITE SAVAGE

tude towards "such solemn matters." Most of the frontiersmen of the day lived violent and lawless lives; those who died professing the True Faith usually had been overtaken by God near the end of their tether—as was the case of the Indian scout, Simon Kenton—or after some terrible adventure in which they had nearly died.

Patriotism, however, was a more general sentiment with the borderers. But here again Simon was deficient in civilized feelings. Though by birth a Pennsylvanian, he sided with the Virginians in the boundary war which came on when Pennsylvania established a Bedford County seat at Hannastown. Bedford had been made from Westmoreland County and included Fort Pitt. But Virginia claimed that Pennsylvania was a thief, having no right to the fort or to some of the land east of it or to much of the territory that stretched westward. All of that belonged to Virginia, Lord Dunmore contended; and with a gesture suited to an earl who was Governor-in-Chief, Captain-General and Vice Admiral of the Colony and Dominion of Virginia, he appointed one John Connolly to make the Pittsburghers dissatisfied with Pennsylvania and clamorous to be taken in under the government of Virginia.

Into this disturbance stepped Simon Girty, not on an impulse, it is likely, but because John Connolly or because Lord Dunmore, who had been at Fort Pitt when the trouble began—in 1773—made him an agreeable offer. But whatever the reasons for his disaffection from Pennsylvania, the fact that he aided Virginia's grasping claims turned him towards the Tories of the country and against the men who wanted to set up a rule of their own. John, Earl of Dunmore, governed his Dominion in the interests of King George and was thoughtful of his commands. John Connolly, as the governor's appointee at Fort Pitt, was likewise a thorough-going loyalist.

Thus the two major events in Simon's growing life were of the kind that set him at variance with the motive of the times. The first was his stay among the Indians, whose point of view he learned so well that he was without sympathy for the land companies that were trying to force westward colonization. The second was his alignment with the Tories, which placed him outside the sweep of independence that was stirring the country.

By Connolly Simon was engaged to help strengthen Virginia's claims in the new territory about Fort Pitt and to aid the settlers in growing used to the new name—Fort Dunmore. There followed violent business at elections and Simon gave good account of his short but brawny arm; once, however, in the name of chivalry. For he not only cracked heads about the Hannastown courthouse; he at one time, during a bitter election, raised his hand to catch a blow aimed by a Virginia partisan at a woman's head.

But the Pennsylvanians were not passive under Dunmore's attempt to annex Fort Pitt. They fought back. There were fights and arrests. Arthur St. Clair, then a justice of the peace for Westmoreland County, had Connolly jailed and signed a warrant for the apprehension of Girty. Connolly, however, was released; he afterward led Virginia militiamen against the Pennsylvania court at Hannastown and ordered the imprisonment of three of its justices. And as for Simon it is doubtful whether he was even captured. He was rather proud of being a law unto himself.

This boundary warfare continued for a year, then was interrupted by more serious trouble. Down along the Ohio a great many white families were being murdered by angry Shawanese and Mingoes. To check these marauds, to restore confidence to the pioneers and to drive the Indians farther westward, Lord Dunmore began the organization of a large force of militiamen to enter the Ohio country where the Shawanese, Mingoes and a few Delawares had their villages.

The Shawanese had been forced to take up a wandering existence and now for the first time in many years were settled. Up to the middle of the eighteenth century they had traveled over most of eastern North Amer-

Tecumseh

ica in search of hunting grounds that were unoccupied and had finally come to rest in what became southern Ohio, where they were permitted to remain by the Wyandots, who had claims to that country. Nearby were mixed groups of Senecas and Delawares. As individuals they had been in conflict with the borderers for some time. On both sides there had been attacks and outrageous murders as a result of two races with opposing purposes and different modes of conduct living so close to each other. Settlers from Virginia went into the Indian territory and established their farms, unchecked by Dinwiddie and, later, Dunmore. And, sometimes through fear and sometimes because they were ruffians, they shot those Indians who got in their way. More than once they killed passive braves, squaws and children.

That had been the fate of the family of Logan, a chief of the Mingo tribe. For years he had been friendly with the borderers, had helped them on occasion; but he was repaid for this by parties of marauding militiamen murdering all of his relations. It maddened him and he went out to kill heartily. It was, superficially, the vengeful work of Logan that brought Lord Dunmore and his army westward.

When Dunmore reached Fort Pitt—or Fort Dunmore as he had it called—on his way down the Ohio

THE WHITE SAVAGE

to join Colonel Andrew Lewis, who had gone ahead towards the mouth of the Great Kanawha in command of half the army of 3,000 men, he enrolled Simon Girty as a scout and interpreter. Theretofore Girty had never been active against the Indians and whether he would have gone had it not been for his service under Dunmore during the boundary trouble is uncertain. For considerably more than a decade he had lived about Pittsburgh and had been in frequent and friendly contact with Delawares, Shawanese and Senecas. Nevertheless he joined Dunmore's army; and with George Rogers Clark, Colonel Cresap, Simon Kenton, John Gibson, William Crawford and a host of others known to western history he left Fort Pitt in August, 1774, in the general movement against the Indians.

The campaign, like most of those that were aimed at the Ohio savages, was poorly managed. Dunmore's original plan was for Colonel Lewis to march westward along the Great Kanawha while his Lordship proceeded down the Ohio from Fort Pitt to the Great Kanawha's mouth, where both divisions were to meet. But this Governor-in-Chief, Captain-General and Vice Admiral of Virginia changed his mind so often after both forces had been put in motion that Lewis reached the designated spot and had to engage the enemy without support—while Dunmore had entirely left the Ohio and was marching half the army through the forest westward, which was directly away from him!

Where the Great Kanawha emptied into the Ohio River a V-shaped piece of land points towards the southwest, the smaller stream running along its lower side, the larger bounding the upper. It was on this strip—Point Pleasant—that Lewis' division was encamped when the Indians under Cornstalk, Blackhoof and Logan surprised them. The Virginia riflemen quickly spread out among the trees in a line nearly two miles wide, their right flanked by the Kanawha, their left by the Ohio. Fighting grew hot immediately, a mass of braves flinging themselves on the right flank, killing Colonel Charles Lewis, the officer in command there, and breaking through at some points. But support came almost at once from Colonels Field and Fleming.

The attack was a morning surprise and Andrew Lewis had made no plans for such an encounter. The Virginians slowly fell back, giving ground inch by inch until the sun had come to the height of its daily course and was beginning to descend. Opposite them Chief Cornstalk urged on his warriors; his voice could be heard above the crackling muskets exclaiming in the Shawanese, "Be strong! Be strong!"

But by early afternoon the Virginians got a footing and with good positions stubbornly held forced the

THE WHITE SAVAGE

warriors to a standstill. Along the front now narrowed down to a mile and a quarter, both flanks guarded by a river bank, they took each other's fire until sundown.

During the night the warriors followed their custom, religiously adhered to, of carrying away the dead and wounded. Their loss was comparatively great, estimated at 233; it was more than a quarter of their whole force. While in the Virginians' camp half the officers were dead or dying and fifty-two enlisted men had been killed. But before morning the Indians disappeared. Though they had worked nearly till dawn they had to leave twenty-one unburied bodies on the ground.

Soon after the battle one of Lord Dunmore's runners arrived with orders for Colonel Lewis to join him at Old Chillicothe, the Shawanese headquarters in what is now Pickaway County, Ohio. The victors of Point Pleasant made their eighty-mile march through the unbroken wilderness and reached the village to find Lord Dunmore listening to peace offers from the Shawanese. For, after the braves had lost, Cornstalk led them directly back to the Chillicothe towns and there called a tribal council. After upbraiding his warriors for not letting him make peace before the engagement (which it appears he had wanted to do) he scolded them, "What will you do now? The Long Knife is coming upon us and we shall all be killed! Now you must fight or we are done." Nobody answered him. He went on desperately, "Then let us kill all our women and our children and go and fight until we die!" Still nobody answered; then burying the blade of his tomahawk in one of the timbers of the council house he exclaimed disgustedly, "I'll go and make peace!" Then when he had finished speaking all the surrounding warriors had nodded their agreement.

But anything more than a sham peace and a flimsy treaty was impossible. Virginia and Pennsylvania were at war over a boundary line that had not been run; King George had recently limited the colonies' western frontier, taking all of the land northwest of the Ohio for Canada; because of the white man's yearning for the Indian's land and the Indian's resentment thereto no lasting agreement could be made until the red men were wholly conquered; and moreover the feeling that there was about to be a revolution was nearly as strong on this edge of the wilderness as along the more populous and more civilized seaboard.

Lord Dunmore returned Cornstalk's messengers with the reply that he was willing to parley. This infuriated Lewis, who, finding himself with twenty-five hundred Virginians well into the Indian country, thought it an excellent moment to destroy the Shawanese completely. He refused to halt while the council gathered, but Dun-

THE WHITE SAVAGE

more "went in person to enforce his orders, and it is said drew his sword upon Colonel Lewis, threatening him with instant death if he persisted in further disobedience." Lewis gave in and the troops were checked; they bivouacked on the ground that Dunmore had named Camp Charlotte.

Soon Shawanese chieftains began to assemble, also a few of the Mingoes. But there was one head warrior that proudly stayed away. It was Logan, whose goodwill the borderers, by their stupidity and reckless murdering, had forfeited. And as no treaty could be concluded without his agreement he was sent for. Lord Dunmore, looking about for an able man, selected Simon Girty.

Girty had remained with Dunmore throughout the advance into the Indian country. Ordered to get Logan's view with regard to the proposed treaty he went, feeling rather reluctant. On his way out of the camp he stopped and talked with one of the pickets whom he told of his mission and also that he disliked it, for Logan, he said, would be in a surly, dangerous mood.

Logan was encountered under a great elm tree, bare against the November sky, which stood some distance from his cabin. There he waited, bronzed, powerful and gloomily fatalistic; stiff with habitual dignity, enwrapped and made perilous by bitter memories of the death of his people, his blood still seething for revenge—that was the kind of man Girty had to meet.

Logan spoke. He began with a kind of harsh mournfulness:

"I appeal to any white man to say if ever he entered Logan's cabin hungry and I gave him not meat; if ever he came cold or naked and I gave him not clothing!

"During the course of the last long and bloody war, Logan remained in his tent, an advocate of peace. Nay, such was my love for the whites that those of my own country pointed at me as they passed and said, 'Logan is the friend of the white man.' I had even thought to live with you, but for the injuries of one man. Colonel Cresap, the last spring, in cold blood and unprovoked, cut off all the relatives of Logan, not sparing even women and children. There runs not a drop of my blood in the veins of any creature. This called on me for revenge. I have sought it. I have killed many. I have fully glutted my vengeance. For my country I rejoice at the beams of peace. Yet do not harbor the thought that mine is the joy of fear. Logan never felt fear. He will not turn on his heel to save his life. Who is there to mourn for Logan? Not one."

He turned away again and the interview was over. Girty marched back to Camp Charlotte with the words ringing in his head. The white men and Indians were seated in a large circle, waiting for the parley to begin. As Girty walked across the crisp grass towards them one of the officers—it was John Gibson—arose and greeted him. Where was Logan? asked Gibson. Girty told him, adding that the parley might now be started, for the Mingo chief had agreed to peace. Did Girty remember what Logan had said? inquired Gibson. Simon nodded; whereupon the two men went into Gibson's tent and there the one repeated to the other the speech, which Gibson set down "on a piece of clean, new paper" that he had in his pocket, the words substantially as Logan had spoken them.

The treaty continued for some days and it was at length decided that—so it had been said by white men—the Indians would thenceforth make the Ohio River their eastern boundary, while the Virginians promised not to pass beyond that river, also that the Shawanese should give Dunmore four of their chiefs to be taken back to Virginia as hostages.

When that meaningless treaty had been concluded the army moved back across the Ohio. Girty accompanied Dunmore and had the satisfaction of being known as a man whose service had been faithful and competent. It is not difficult to imagine him, while leading the advance towards Camp Charlotte, thrusting his way through trees and underbrush, leading the army into the wilderness he knew so well, assisting in gaining intelligence from captured Indians and acting as interpreter and messenger when the parley began. That he was looked on favorably by Dunmore is certain: while both branches of the army were marching towards the Indian country he had been chosen as one of the messengers to Colonel Andrew Lewis; and after the trouble-breeding treaty at the Chillicothe town it was Girty whom the noble Virginia governor called on to provide amusement for the officers.

An Indian dance was what Lord Dunmore wanted to see. Girty arranged it. With young John Turner and the two Nicholson brothers he led his sham warriors shouting and pounding the earth with their moccasins about a campfire in a clearing; they sang the weird, dolorous Indian songs, gave out their fearful yells and loudly thumped a skin-topped drum that was half full of water. His Lordship was greatly pleased. And when the army reached Fort Pitt Simon was given a commission in Dunmore's militia.

As a second lieutenant in the battalion commanded by Major John Connolly, Girty was required to swear away any lingering belief of transubstantiation in the sacrament of the Lord's Supper and to give full allegiance to his Majesty, King George the Third. He complied, his right hand upraised, on February 22,

THE WHITE SAVAGE

1775, a day not far distant from the eighteenth of April, same year.

Had there been no particular occurrence on that eighteenth of April and had it not been a step towards the Revolutionary War, the life of Simon Girty would have been vastly changed. There would probably have been no tales about "Girty, the White Indian"; "Girty, the White Savage"; no legends of his ferocious cruelty and indignant accounts of his barbarous deeds and bloody nature. It is likely he would have remained about Pittsburgh, going no higher than a captaincy in the militia, or would have made it a base for his job as scout and interpreter to the parties venturing among the Indians in the wilderness. For he seems to have had no markedly acquisitive instinct and no strong urge to rise up to a position above his fellows.

But the Revolution was at hand even as he swore the oath of loyalty to King George. Washington had written to Bryan Fairfax, "as to your political sentiments, I would heartily join you in them, so far as relates to a humble and dutiful petition to the throne, provided there was the most distant hope of success. But have we not tried this already? Have we not addressed the Lords, and remonstrated with the commons? And to what end? Did they deign to look at our petitions? Does it not appear, as clear as the sun in its meridian brightness, that there is a regular, systematic plan formed to fix the right and practice of taxation upon us?" And at a Fairfax County meeting the next month Washington offered to raise and equip a thousand soldiers and send them to the aid of Boston.

Also there were men farther west in Virginia who felt the struggle coming on and, realizing that Lord Dunmore was no friend of the colonists, were anxious to dispossess King George's governor. While Dunmore was with his army at the Hocking River on his expedition against the Shawanese and Mingoes one of the soldiers saw the commander sitting in his tent with two Indians. Upon which he conceived the idea of killing not only Dunmore but the redskin guests with one shot. Circling the tent, the soldier paused and fired through the canvas. But because of his greed he missed all three, then quickly hid among the rank and file, none of whom would tell who had fired the ball. "From the time he left the camp," wrote one of the men who had been on the expedition, "Dunmore tried to conciliate what he could by indulgence and talking; but this would not have availed him had he not taken other precautions, for many in the camp believed him the enemy of their country and the betrayer of the army."

Some of this feeling is expressed in a resolution drawn up by Dunmore's officers at Camp Charlotte where the treaty with the Indians was held. In its preamble it summed up the campaign against the Shawanese and Mingoes as having been successful (which it was not), asserted that the assembled army was a respectable body, that it had lived for weeks without either bread or salt and that its men could march and shoot with any in the known world. "Blessed with these talents," goes on this extraordinary document, "let us solemnly engage to one another and our country in particular that we will use them for no other purpose but for the honor and advantage of America and of Virginia in particular. It behooves us, then, for the satisfaction of our country, that we should give them our real sentiments by way of resolves, in this very alarming crisis." Whereupon all of the officers promised to bear the most faithful allegiance to King George so long as "his majesty delights to reign over a brave and free people" and further resolved that they felt "the greatest respect for his excellency the Rt. Hon. Lord Dunmore, who commanded the expedition against the Shawanese, and who, we are confident, underwent the greatest fatigue of this singular campaign from no other motive than the true interests of his country."

But whatever Lord Dunmore's motives were in the campaign, it is true that he foresaw grievous trouble between the colonies and Great Britain and that he labored to recruit and strengthen loyalists to the King's government. And in this he had the assistance of Connolly at Fort Pitt.

Connolly, in those days before the fracas at Concord and Lexington, either under instruction from Lord Dunmore or on his account, provided the Virginia governor with a list of names of people about the Virginia frontier who, he believed, were well-disposed towards British rule. It contained descriptions of nineteen men, Indians, traders and frontiersmen, and was sent by Connolly to Dunmore, by Dunmore to Lord George Germain and by Germain to Sir Guy Carleton, governor-general of Quebec—a piece of paper evidently regarded as being of great importance. But though this list was to be handed from one bigwig to another almost any piece of paper picked up at random would have been as valuable to the British government.

For of the nineteen named nearly all took up the side of the colonials when war came. Included in the list were Major (later Colonel) William Crawford, who commanded Pennsylvania militiamen during the Revolution; White Eyes, a chief of the Delawares whose personal efforts kept half his tribe from joining the Senecas against the Americans; the bereaved Logan, who never from 1774 lifted his arm against the white men, and Cornstalk, a chieftain of the Shawanese who was also friendly towards the frontiersmen. In fact the only men Connolly could have relied upon that were mentioned in the list were Alexander McKee and Simon Girty.

During the first years of the war Simon moved with the patriotic tide about Fort Pitt. Connolly's militia had been withdrawn and Girty was left without either commission or job. There was no more talk of calling the place Fort Dunmore. For the Virginia governor was no longer a power there; it was Fort Pitt and Pittsburgh and belonged to Pennsylvania! The frontiersmen spoke little about boundary lines or even about Indians; their conversation was chiefly concerned with affairs along the distant seaboard.

Shifting about in this changed scene, Simon finally went to work as an interpreter for George Morgan, the new deputy commissioner of Indian Affairs. But he was given odd jobs, small pay and little encouragement. It was not the same as when he had worked with Alexander McKee, deputy agent of Indian Affairs under the Crown; with Major Connolly and Lord Dunmore. Under Morgan, however, he made several journeys into the Ohio country, also one for the Virginia House of Burgesses. But he got on badly with his superior and within three months he was discharged. To lose his job was a thing of little importance in itself. So was the fact that when he presented his bill for about a hundred dollars which he had expended in "extraordinary service"—one item being "a horse taken by Mr. George Morgan and given out in the service of the public"—the bill was not paid. But he had not had trouble like that under the old rule.

During the next two years while ragged troops were maneuvering in the east, fighting under Washington at Trenton, Germantown, Brandywine and at last going into winter quarters at Valley Forge, Girty tried to fit himself into the new scheme of things as manifested at Pittsburgh. There, since June of 1777, Brigadier General Edward N. Hand was in command. And whether it was because the frontiersmen of that neighborhood were suspicious of any man who had been an officer under Connolly and Lord Dunmore, or because Simon associated with Alexander McKee, then on parole to the Continental government, or whether it was simply his continued familiarity with the Indians—whatever the reason, it was rumored that he was in league with McKee to slay all the Americans on the border. Though such a claim sounds obviously like nonsense, there may have been at the base of it some fact that showed him indifferent to the cause of the United States. At any rate he was jailed on the charge (breaking out of the guardhouse, he absented himself a few days, then returned and gave himself up, evidently to show his independence), but when brought to trial there was no proof that could be brought against him.

In a time of disturbance, such as a great social upheaval, when men of one belief are thrown out while those of another take their place, there is bound to be great dissatisfaction with whatever may occur in the reorganized society. One ambitious soul is stirred, only to be hampered and suspected by countless others. That was the fate of Arnold, one of the bravest and most competent generals in the Continental army; the fate of Anthony Wayne, an excellent drill-master, deeply engrossed in the military life and personally valiant, who had to stand aside while his inferiors as soldiers but his betters as politicians were given the appointments that should have gone to him; and, in a lesser degree, to be sure, that was likewise the misfortune of Girty.

A man with Girty's peculiar qualifications should have been of inestimable value to Pennsylvania and Virginia on the western edge of the wilderness during the War of the Revolution. He knew the country northwest of the Ohio as well as any white man at Fort Pitt. He had an understanding of the Indians, their manners and speech and the land they occupied. He was courageous and outspoken. His interest in private property (he was never known to have been a trader or to stake out land claims, either of which he might easily have done) was small. Hence at Fort Pitt he could have been depended on to make true reports of the temper and wants of the Shawanese, Wyandots and Delawares, to conciliate them if that were possible, not to steal from them as did so many of the Indian agents, and to plan expeditions, at least the routes that were to be taken, when that was necessary.

Nor was it unlikely he would have given such service if he had had the chance. Throughout 1777 he had worked on behalf of the colonists, recruiting men of the settlements for the army under one-year enlistments. How many men he brought in or how heartily he worked is not known, but he must have been fairly successful. And for what he had done he expected a captaincy.

In this he was disappointed. John Stephenson was put in command of the company and Girty's reward was a second lieutenancy. That was the rank he had held under Connolly, and men who had been lieutenants and captains then were now majors and colonels. Moreover, he discovered, the company was to be sent to Charleston. It was too hot down there. Not wanting to go to Charleston, he remained at Fort Pitt and a short time later was out of a job again.

These small but repeated failures disgruntled him.

THE WHITE SAVAGE

During the rest of the year at Pittsburgh he was seen as often with visiting Indians as with his own kind.

Another man who had grievances against the revolutionaries was Alexander McKee. He was a man of substance and had servants on his plantation down the river. Not only had the rebellion cost him his position as Indian Agent and caused him to be placed on parole as a person suspected of seditious sentiments, but his Tory sympathies had raised a popular clamor against him. He was charged with violating his parole, and though tried and acquitted the suspicion still remained. On February 7, 1778, General Hand ordered him to go at once "to Yorktown, in Penn., on your parole, there to receive the further directions of the Hon. Continental Board of War."

But by this time McKee had decided that if he left Fort Pitt at all—his property was there—it would be to go in another direction. Drawn together by their dissatisfaction with affairs as they had now become, McKee and Girty, with Matthew Elliott, a young Irish trader who had been much with the Indians, McKee's cousin Robert Surphlit, "a man named Higgins" and two of McKee's Negro servants planned their departure for Detroit, where they intended to offer themselves to General Henry Hamilton, Lieutenant-Governor of Canada.

From there, for nearly twenty years Girty, McKee

and Elliott were ably to direct Ohio Indians in the border war, to keep the frontier from encroaching far into the Northwest and to help prolong the fight between Great Britain and America over the land south of Lake Erie and northwest of the Ohio River.

Wherein the Scoundrel Saves a Hero from Roasting at the Stake

CHAPTER IV

Wherein the Scoundrel Saves a Hero from Roasting at the Stake

*F*AIRNESS and level-headedness are qualities not often found in accounts of that long drawn out fight for supremacy in the country northwest of the Ohio River. Western historians have generally taken for granted that all of the land in North America belonged by divine right to the offspring of the Thirteen Colonies and that any attempt by the Indians to drive back the settlers was cruel, treacherous and extraordinarily criminal. And the frontiersmen who successfully gained a footing within Shawanese or Delaware country were said to have "met their dastardly, cruel, relentless foe in the spirit of genuine manhood—of true, determined, unflinching heroism!" and were called "men worthy of the heroic age of the west."

That land in which several small white armies foundered, but which the braves finally had to relinquish, was worth the blood that moistened it. To the white settlers it gave various ores, pottery, rich fields and timber. To the Indian it supplied his every want. Its rivers, though small, were many and navigable by pirogue, raft and canoe. Fish were large and plentiful in all the streams, caught merely by the throwing of a spear near the flashing shallows or by the dipping of a net near the shade of an overhanging willow. The game was abundant. There were fat but surprisingly agile bears, slim-flanked deers, raccoon, wild turkeys, buffaloes, and groundhog for the not too fastidious. And in killing a bear or deer the brave got not only meat for his family but clothing and bedding and skins for his cabin as well. For his vegetables and corn he had but to scratch the ground in the river bottoms and plant the seed after the water had subsided from the perennial spring thaws.

Why the Indian fought to keep his land in the Ohio country is obvious: it contained everything that he needed; and once driven from it there was little place else for him to go. The tribes were of a wandering nature, it is true; nevertheless each division of the aborigines had its own territory in which it alone had the right to live and hunt. Through the summer the braves would remain close by their villages; in the winter they would go forth with musket and bow and arrow to less frequented forests where the bear and deer were not so wary. But as for wandering further, they abandoned

THE SCOUNDREL SAVES A HERO

their villages only when the land and surrounding wilderness failed to support them.

In the Ohio country the tribes had a fairly settled existence. To the north and east were Wyandots and Delawares, to the south the Shawanese, with the Miamis along the western boundary. Among these the Shawanese were the most recent arrivals, having come there in the middle of the eighteenth century. Nearly a hundred years earlier they had journeyed from the south, perhaps from Florida, and had been permitted by the Seneca-Iroquois confederacy to build towns on the Susquehanna. But later, by the treaty with William Penn in 1682, they were required to decamp. And after gipsying through Virginia, South Carolina and Tennessee, going clear to the Mississippi where La Salle found them in 1684, they turned back and, this time with permission of the Wyandots, settled in southern Ohio near and along the Scioto River. Thus they had been buffeted considerably since the white man had come to America. Scarcely had they reared their cabins on the Scioto when they discovered that Virginians and North Carolinians had penetrated the friendly forests as far as the Ohio's shores. It angered them and they could not but wonder how long it would be before they were driven on again. Lord Dunmore's war a few decades after their arrival not only restricted their boundary to the south and east; it also showed them the temper of the frontiersmen, who, in general, killed as treacherously and with as little regard for age and sex as the Shawanese brave himself.

Of all the Indian tribes in the Ohio country the position of the Shawanese was the most precarious. They had come but recently; they were under sufferance of the Wyandots, and it was the fringe of their hunting grounds that was the most exposed to the westward pushing pioneers. Second to them, so far as the danger of conflict was concerned, were the Delawares.

Contact with Europeans had sent the Shawanese wandering to the south; it had driven the Delawares directly west from the seaboard at a much earlier period. They had never been, and they never were, great warriors. Thir right to live in the Ohio country came from the Senecas, who long before this western continent had been heard of had defeated them in battle and by some strategy had managed to hold them in an inferior position. They continued at intervals to humiliate them. Compared to the bold and forthright Shawanese, the Delawares were an almost indecently wobbly tribe. Their noted warriors were few—Hopocan, or Captain Pipe as he was called, being about the best they could furnish at any time during the last half of the eighteenth century. Their sachems were insignificant in the inter-

THE SCOUNDREL SAVES A HERO

tribal councils. Though the braves would fight, and often did fight, the spirit of blood revenge, so strong in the Indians as a whole, was weak in them. All this, however, in no way lessened their aptitude towards cruelty to captives.

Coincident with the westward urge along the frontier came the spirit of organized soul saving. While borderers tried hard but none too successfully to tame the braves with long squirrel rifles there were other white men ready to conquer the warrior in the wilderness with nothing but the Word of God. So far as is known the work of the missionaries among the Ohio Indians was not, for the most part, fruitful. The Shawanese, Miamis, and nearly all of the Wyandots preferred their old familiar ways of worship. These permitted an invalid to recover by giving a great feast in honor of the Sun God. They also insured the steady capture of game by the hunter; he had only to cajole the souls of the dead beasts which his people had already consumed.

But one John Heckewelder and some of his Christian brothers, going into the midst of the Delawares, succeeded in making numerous conversions to the Methodist religion. Heckewelder was a stubborn, flighty-headed man born in England of German parentage. He had come to Pennsylvania as a youth and was soon obsessed with theological mysteries. Northwest of Fort

THE WHITE SAVAGE

Pitt along the Muskingum River he preached Christianity to those who would listen and after a time he helped establish three Indian missions. One of them was called Salem, another Schönbrunn, and the third was Gnadenhutten. There he instructed the Delawares in building more weatherproof cabins, cultivating the clearings and bottomlands and in saving up their stores for days when food was hard to get. But while shepherding a flock of several hundred Indians he took care to keep well in the good graces of the Continental officers at Fort Pitt.

Heckewelder, with another missionary named Joseph Bull, was at Fort Pitt a few days after Simon Girty, Alexander McKee and Matthew Elliott disappeared into the wilderness. Since these three had gone, he observed, the faces of the pioneers, their wives and children were dark with gloom; they were fearful of their fate and ready to bundle up their few belongings and return east. General Hand was blenched with consternation and so was Colonel John Gibson. The Pittsburghers looked to them for safety, for they believed that Girty, McKee and Elliott would shortly return at the head of a howling warpack and put them to the death.

But Heckewelder, thereby heroizing himself, was not so easily shaken; and he set out for the Muskingum to counteract this evil to the American cause. Arriving

THE SCOUNDREL SAVES A HERO

at Salem he discovered that though these three runaways had been there they had moved on. Before leaving they had represented the colonists as having been beaten and the British triumphant, which had wakened the Delawares to thoughts of attacking the frontier. But brave Heckewelder, prepared with newspapers (it is curious how apt the Indians were at reading English) and some friendly speeches, soon proved to them that it was the British who had suffered the defeats and cited Burgoyne's fate at Saratoga. This turn of affairs moved Chief White Eyes to send a message to the Shawanese on the Scioto—where the three white men had journeyed—saying, "Grandchildren, ye Shawanese! Some days ago a flock of birds from the East lit at [Coshocton], imposing a song of theirs upon us, which song had nigh proved our ruin! Should these birds, which, on leaving us, took their flight toward the Scioto, endeavor to impose a song on you likewise, do not listen to them, for they lie."

What kind of song these birds sang among the Shawanese is not known. But likely enough whatever the tune it was one the tribe had learned by heart. For they were aware that already they were half surrounded, by Pennsylvanians and Virginians to the east, and to the south by settlers who had followed Daniel Boone, the Harrods, McAfees, Hendersons, Floyds, Hancocks,

THE WHITE SAVAGE

Bullets and others into Kentucky. They knew they would have to fight, and they had chieftains like Cornstalk, Blackhoof, Blue Jacket, Red Hawk and, later, Tecumseh, who were competent and who, with the exception of Cornstalk, were eager to lead them.

Certain it is that Girty and his companions spoke no good for the colonists. But it would appear if not also certain at least reasonable that this party of white men in going among the Shawanese intended no direct harm towards the borderers, but rather went there for refuge until they should hear from Lieutenant-Governor Hamilton in Detroit. For McKee had written Hamilton while they were at the Delaware village of Coshocton asking for a safeguard through the territory of the western tribes. By way of reply Hamilton had sent out Edward Hazle to the Scioto to escort them back through the Indian country.

The three had escaped from Fort Pitt late in March. It was June before they arrived in Detroit, where Hamilton eagerly awaited them. For he had got the list of names which Connolly had made for Dunmore and which had gone through Lord George Germain to Sir Guy Carleton, and the list showed McKee and Girty to be men of influence and well-disposed towards the British government. They fitted in to Hamilton's plans exactly. Because by this time he had received official

THE SCOUNDREL SAVES A HERO

sanction of the plan he had put forward, namely the harassing of the American frontier by Indians whom men of his own choice were to lead. He was anxious for the Wyandot and Shawanese warriors to be at their work, wheeling efficiently down upon the stockades in Kentucky, Pennsylvania and Virginia.

Hamilton welcomed the runaways. And after they had been in Detroit a while he spoke to them of the jobs he wanted them to do. They were to go down into the Ohio country and live among the Indians, interpreting for the traders among them and keeping them friendly towards the British, seeing that the presents given the tribes from the King's stores reached them safely and, on occasion, leading the braves against the American settlements.

This last part of their task, Hamilton might have pointed out to them, was not so unnatural and bloodthirsty as it sounded. The Indians were making marauds upon the border anyway; they might as well be properly led. Besides, the white men who accompanied them were required to restrain the braves from unnecessary cruelty (as if that were humanly possible!) and to hold them back from killing women and children.

The three men took up their new employment. Soon afterward Simon, as his first assignment, was sent to the mixed-up tribe called Mingoes. He reached their

THE WHITE SAVAGE

villages from Detroit by following the Indian trail down the Detroit River, skirting the west shore of Lake Erie, crossing the Maumee River near the rapids and going on through the wilderness towards the headwaters of the Scioto. Here he found them occupying the small area that lay surrounded by the Miamis to the west, the Wyandots to the north and east and the Shawanese to the south.

His meeting with the Mingoes was friendly. They understood that it was through him that they would receive their annual presents from the King's stores and be supplied with provisions and gunpowder for their raids against the border. It was not necessary for him to win them to a new point of view. He had merely to keep them reminded that the Great White Father across the water was really their parent, that he was all-powerful and good, whereas the Long Knives of Pennsylvania and Virginia were not powerful and not good.

Simon settled among them in Solomon's town, which was a few miles upward from the Shawanese village of Wapatomica. There he built a stout log cabin which had a roof of bark and which he furnished with a bed made from bent saplings, perhaps a stool or two and the skins of bear and deer.

Altogether he found his situation agreeable. The necessaries of life were free for the taking. He was

THE SCOUNDREL SAVES A HERO

receiving regular pay from General Hamilton. The Indians gave him the respect they would have given to one of their war chiefs. He talked with them and understood them enough neither to overestimate nor to belittle what they were. They came to his cabin and were his friends.

While Simon was living at Solomon's town his brother James broke away from the Americans and went to Detroit where Hamilton hired him as an interpreter and sent him down among the Shawanese. Simon met James a short time later and James told him of a raid the Shawanese were planning against the Kentucky border. They wanted him to accompany them.

He went. Riding a well-equipped horse and leading two packmares, he set out with the braves as one of the "proper persons . . . to conduct their parties, and, restrain[ing] them from committing violence on the well-affected and Inoffensive inhabitants, employ[ed] them in making a Diversion and exciting an alarm upon the frontier."

Gone for two weeks or more, the party returned with some plunder, a white woman, seven children and a handful of scalps which they had taken from some poorly stockaded settlement in a Kentucky clearing. And as Simon, more or less the leader or the party, reached Wapatomica he met the first of his old Fort

THE WHITE SAVAGE

Pitt acquaintances whom he was destined to see under trying circumstances.

Among the scouts that had worked with Girty in Lord Dunmore's war was Simon Kenton, a young, blond, broad-faced six-footer. They were friends of a sort, the two Simons. But while one of them had deserted his people at Fort Pitt and aligned himself against them, the other had been drawn more closely to the American frontiersman's side. Kenton had gone with George Rogers Clark to take Vincennes and had also skirmished with the Indians under Daniel Boone. But in this summer of 1778 he was lying idly about Boone's Station and, likely enough, thinking enviously of the Shawanese with their horses on the other side of the Ohio River. At any rate the Shawanese had horses which would be very acceptable to the settlers at Boone's Station and Kenton determined that a transfer in their ownership should be made. With Alexander Montgomery and George Clark he set out one fine day to get them, taking the salt and bridles necessary to the capture.

The three adventurers—they couldn't be called horse thieves because, after all, they were only taking the property from the Indians—crossed the Ohio and on the following night came upon a herd of horses grazing in a natural meadow. In the darkness they caught and slipped halters on seven of them, then started back

Simon Kenton

THE SCOUNDREL SAVES A HERO

towards the river. By dawn they had come to the wood-fringed shore without mishap and none of them doubted that the rest of the trip back to Boone's Station would be as successful as had been the first part of the journey.

But a wind was blowing over the wide stretch of water, sending the waves high up on the muddy banks. The stolen horses took fright; rearing and tossing their heads, they would not attempt the crossing.

By noon the whipped-up surface had not subsided. There stood three anxious and angry men and seven rebellious horses. Meanwhile in the forest behind them the Indians to whom the stock belonged had discovered their loss and had already begun to track them.

At last, the horses refusing to take to the water, Kenton, Montgomery and Clark led them to the path that followed the shore line and went westward, towards the falls where, if it could be reached, there would be an easy crossing.

But before they had gone very far they heard the sounds of Shawanese behind them. The three men scattered, letting the horses roam; Kenton ran down through a stretch of timber where many trees had been blown down. Coming out on the other side he was faced by a mounted Indian who slipped off his horse and ran upon him with tomahawk uplifted. Kenton took up his musket as a cudgel, was about to defend himself when another brave leaped upon his back and shoulders and pinioned his arms. The tomahawk was stayed; Kenton gave up and was bound with leather thongs.

During this time Clark had escaped and Montgomery had been shot. Indians came to where the tall blond captive stood and one of them showed him Montgomery's scalp and shook it in his face as a warning. Heeding it, he remained passive in their hands. His position, he must have known, was grave indeed. He had come to steal Shawanese horses and had been caught at it, had attempted to escape and had been overpowered. Moreover, his brawn made him a prize to be carefully guarded while being taken back to the Indian village before the sachems and braves who would decide as to the manner of his death.

The following morning Kenton was tied to a fractious horse. Prone on its back, he was lashed by one rope that bound his neck to that of the mount, by another that held his ankles together under its belly and by still another that cuffed his wrists. While a brave drew moccasins over the prisoner's hands to prevent him from warding off any of the stinging brush that would slap and scratch him as the horse cantered through the wilderness, the others stood hilariously about and jeeringly asked him if he thought he would ever come again among the Shawanese to steal their horses. They then

THE SCOUNDREL SAVES A HERO

all set off. And the horse, after wildly kicking and plunging to free itself of its heavy burden, amiably followed the party on its return.

On the painful journey Kenton might have held some hope for his life being spared by captors grown merciful at the sight of his fortitude. But that was all there was to cheer him. For escape was impossible. During the day he was trussed to the horse; at night the braves took him down and stretched him on the ground with his legs extended wide, then fastened each member to a stake driven in the ground. Added to that a pole was laid across his chest and his outstretched arms strapped to it with thongs. Another rope, tied to a nearby sapling, encircled his neck.

Three days and nights of this brought him to Chillicothe, a few miles from which a great horde of youths and warriors, having heard of the prisoner's approach, came out to welcome him with jeers and kicks. They had a great to-do. They danced and sang about him until they grew bored with that form of amusement and returned to their village, leaving him tied in the wilderness for the night.

In the morning, however, they came back. Kenton soon discovered that he was fated to run the gauntlet. Armed with hickory clubs, they formed a long double row and stood waiting while his bonds were loosed and

THE WHITE SAVAGE

he was taken to the beginning of this aisle that extended between two lines of glowering warriors. If the clubs felled him, he knew as he stood there chafing his wrists, he was almost sure to be beaten to death; if he broke through and reached the farther end still on his feet he might hope that there would be some who would later, in the council, plead that mercy be shown him. That possibility for life and also another flickered through his mind as he stood rubbing his neck and his wrists where the thongs had abraded the skin: if he could break through the line and reach the council house in the distant village without being captured his swiftness might win him forgiveness.

He began to run, desperately spurred by the flaying hickory sticks. They struck his head and back and shoulders, made a clatter as they knocked against each other, but still he remained upright. Then of a sudden he saw through the nave of sticks ahead of him the flash of a scalping knife and he knew that at least one brave was bent on his death. With no way of warding off the stroke he took the one big chance. Swerving, he bucked through the line and stretched his legs towards the council house in the village.

He kept his pursuers well behind him as he ran on, hastened by their baying voices. But luck was against him. Winded, though within sight of the council

THE SCOUNDREL SAVES A HERO

house, his path took him directly towards an Indian who unexpectedly appeared from behind a tree. It was too late to dodge. Exhausted, he grappled with the warrior and was thrown on his back as the cries of the pursuing braves closed over him. Above him there was a mêlée: hands ripped at the remnant of his buckskin clothing, moccasins kicked at him and hickory clubs were held in readiness for whacking blows.

After a while they left him there. They came back later and brought food and water so that he might live during the trial which was now being prepared for him in the house that he had failed to reach.

As he lay there recovering from the blows an old chief was seated beneath the skin and bark covered tent poles of the council house. He held a knife in one hand and a stick of wood in the other and around him was a circle of warriors. Kenton was brought into this scene to listen to the arguments for and against his death.

They began speaking in an orderly manner, each addressing the others on the fate of the prisoner. There were those who spoke for clemency, but for the most part the words of the braves were angry and their gestures abrupt and fierce. Then the final speech was made and the old chief in the center calmly lifted up a war club and handed it to an Indian who stood near the door. The club was the ballot and was passed about the circle. One brave thumped it on the ground; that was a vote for Kenton's death and the old chief in the middle made a mark in the earth with his knife. Another, refusing to drop the club, handed it on to his neighbor, and that was a vote against the execution. The old chief thoughtfully marked with his stick of wood.

But when the war club had been handed completely around the circle a large number of scrawls had been made by the knife and only a few with the little hickory stick. Kenton was doomed. The sentence of death was passed and, with this settled, the warriors began to discuss where and when it should take place. Hot-blooded ones were vehement for instant execution, but calmer warriors felt that the execution of this prisoner should be a tribal event. As the latter were of the majority, it was decided that Kenton should be taken to Wapatomica, the town where the chief sachem of the Shawanese had his cabin.

He was removed from the Chillicothe town and carried on a tour of exhibition among the various families that made up his captors' tribe. At Piqua and at the Mackachack towns he again had to run the gauntlet. Little hope of life was left him when he finally reached Wapatomica, where he submitted to the final form that preceded death: his face was blacked, the mark of a condemned prisoner.

THE SCOUNDREL SAVES A HERO

It was while Kenton lay within sight of the stake that Simon Girty came to Wapatomica on his way northward from his raid into Kentucky. With him were his brother James and John Ward, another white man; also some Indians, prisoners and scalps. Coming into Kenton's presence, Girty did not at first recognize his old acquaintance. He saw merely a large-sized man lying on the ground with his hands and feet bound; a man with a blackened face, powerless and doomed. Girty only glanced at him.

But afterward, when he had talked to the Shawanese chiefs about the raid, he stood before Kenton again and started bullyragging him and questioning him with regard to the number of men under arms in Kentucky.

Kenton knew who was talking to him, but cannily kept that knowledge to himself. However, he answered Girty's questions. But finally Girty said, "What's your name and where do you come from?"

Kenton replied with the name by which Girty knew him and which he had used for several years, since, in fact, he had got into a shooting scrape in Virginia and had believed, though falsely, that he had killed his adversary. He said, "Simon Butler."

Abruptly Girty changed. The overbearing tone died away and he stared with wonder at the blackened face before him. "Oh, Butler, my dear friend!" he broke out and, rushing forward, he put his arms around Kenton's shoulders. Suddenly as the two men stood together Girty began to cry unrestrainedly.

After the shock of the encounter had worn off Girty told Kenton slowly that there was little hope of saving him from the stake since the council had passed the sentence, but that he would do whatever he possibly could to influence the warriors. The two men then drew apart and Girty went to the tribal chiefs, asking that they meet in the council house at once so that he could address them.

They came. And in the presence of Kenton he began speaking to the assembly. He talked long and with vehemence, telling them that if they were ever minded to favor him they should show it then and save the life of his friend Kenton. Whatever else he said is not known, for he spoke, of course, in the Shawanese tongue, a language which Kenton did not understand. But at any rate his plea was successful, and, when he had concluded, the Indians "with one simultaneous grunt of approbation spared the prisoner's life and placed him under the care and protection of his old companion, Girty."

But that was far from being the end. The two men went to the British trading post at Wapatomica, where Girty bought Kenton a new outfit of clothing and

THE SCOUNDREL SAVES A HERO

a horse and saddle. Kenton now was free to go, but he remained in the neighborhood and while he was there more danger threatened.

From Wapatomica they rode to Girty's cabin at Solomon's town. Here they stayed, hunting in the surrounding forest, sitting in the dim light of evening while they reviewed their lives in monosyllables. Girty was troubled about having left Fort Pitt. He should not, he said, have gone away like that. But . . . well, he had worked hard trying to get that gang of Pittsburgh roustabouts into a company. He had hoped for a captaincy out of it. Maybe if he had got the captaincy he'd have stayed on there and fought. But Stephenson had got it instead. Well, it was too late to talk about it now.

And Kenton said that it was kind of nice around Solomon's town. The Indians, they weren't so ornery when you got to know them. He didn't stand in well with the government back in Virginia either. Shot a man over a girl and the damn fool died. Now he had to use another name and stay out in Kentucky. Maybe he wouldn't go back at all. Maybe he'd stay right where he was.

But while the two men were living in Girty's cabin in security a party of Shawanese warriors who had made a humiliating foray against Wheeling and had been severely beaten came back to Wapatomica. Several of their warriors had been killed; their comrades returned in a fury and riding up to the council house demanded that the horse-stealing Long Knife be brought back for another trial so that they might have a victim for their wrath.

This word was at once sent out by messenger from Wapatomica to Solomon's town. Meanwhile the two friends had left their cabin and were riding over the same trail on which the runner with the bad news was headed. They met him soon and Girty very shortly knew that the security which the council had given Kenton had been withdrawn. For the gloomy bearer of the message accepted Girty's hand, but disdained to greet Kenton. Then Girty asked the runner the meaning of this hostility. Receiving no answer, he drew him aside and they talked a few moments. Turning from the Indian to Kenton, Girty said that they all would have to go to the council. The three men rode silently down through the wilderness trail to Wapatomica.

The council house was crowded with blanket-enwrapped braves who gave their hands to Girty but scowled at his tall companion. Almost immediately the warriors formed a circle and sat down. Soon they were listening to the chief who had commanded the unsuccessful Wheeling foray. He made jerky gestures and talked fiercely, keeping his ugly eyes on Kenton. Clearly he was asking for the white man's death.

But when the chief had finished Girty jumped to his feet and began to talk earnestly, half pleading and half haranguing. They knew, he told these assembled warriors, of his interest in the Indian's right to the Ohio country and of his efforts to keep it in their hands; they knew of his life and deeds with them, that during the time he had been with them he had fought faithfully and bravely. Now he asked again that the life of his friend be spared.

The council heard him respectfully, then turned to vehement chiefs who kept to their argument that this young man was a hated Long Knife who had come among them to steal their horses and that he should be killed, burned at the stake, as was the custom of disposing of publicly condemned prisoners. After long deliberation the council agreed and Kenton was doomed a second time.

So Girty lost his plea. But he did not yet give up; and in the hope that with time he might find more powerful interference with the Indians' decision against Kenton he asked that the execution be postponed and the prisoner be taken to Upper Sandusky where the eastern Ohio tribes were accustomed to gather to receive their presents from the British government agents at

THE WHITE SAVAGE

Detroit. For if this were agreed to, argued Girty, the burning of the blond six-footer could be turned into a spectacle that great hosts of Indian families could enjoy.

That was what he told the Indians, but what he must have been thinking was that at Upper Sandusky there were British traders who would certainly do what they could to save Kenton from the stake, that there, also, the Indians to whom the prisoner was to be intrusted would have no directly personal feeling towards him and so could be the more easily persuaded in the direction of leniency. Then, too, along the trail between Wapatomica and Upper Sandusky was the Scioto village where Logan lived; and quixotic Logan had long been known as a friend of unfortunate white prisoners in the Ohio country.

In asking this Girty got what he wanted. The council approved Upper Sandusky as the scene of execution and under the guard of five stalwart braves Kenton was that day taken on his journey. And it happened that because of his removal he was saved. At the Scioto town Logan interceded for him (though unsuccessfully), but at Upper Sandusky Peter Druyer, a Canadian trader in the British service, under the pretext that the prisoner possessed military secrets which, if heard at Detroit, would be of value to both Indians and British, and on payment of a hundred dollars' worth of rum and

THE SCOUNDREL SAVES A HERO

tobacco, effected his transfer from the savages to the guardhouse in Detroit.

The council house at Wapatomica was the place where the two adventurous Simons met for the last time, though both were to roam the greater part of the Ohio wilderness throughout the next thirty years. Kenton, in words that sound a little strange, but which, according to McClung, he dictated, used long afterward to end his recollections of Girty with, "but he was good to me; and it was no wonder. When we see our fellow-creatures every day, we don't care for them; but it is different when you meet a man all alone in the woods—the wild, lonely woods."

It was in these woods among the savages that Girty spent the best years of his life.

Simon Becomes Morose; His Scalp Causes Him Some Concern

CHAPTER V

Simon Becomes Morose; His Scalp Causes Him Some Concern

*T*HOUGH the Ohio Indians had good cause to strike at the borderers and though their feelings of jealousy and revenge were deliberately sharpened by Lieutenant-Governor Hamilton, Alexander McKee, Matthew Elliott and Simon Girty, a great number of the savages remained friendly towards the settlers of Pennsylvania, Virginia and Kentucky. For the Indians were a divided, individualistic people and the brave used his right to do what he thought best. Not only did each tribe function independently of the others, but each division and subdivision as well was allowed to decide for itself in matters of war. Moreover, when a petty chief, intent on setting out in a maraud, struck the war pole with his hatchet his braves had the choice of following his action or of remaining in their cabins with their squaws and old men.

This explains why it was that Chief Cornstalk, who led the Shawanese against Lord Dunmore in 1774, could, in 1778, while the bulk of his tribe were actively hostile against the Long Knives, be at peace with his late enemies and willing to prove to them his friendship. It also explains how half the Delawares could engage to fight on the side of the British while the other half favored the Americans. But as for the depressing results of this good will, they can only be explained by the stupidity of the frontiersmen and their leaders.

The same year Simon Girty helped Kenton elude the stake, old Chief Cornstalk, learning that a band of warriors of his tribe were planning an attack upon a Kentucky stockade and being anxious to preserve peace and save the white men from a surprise assault, crossed the Ohio to warn the garrison. He arrived with the information and delivered it, then started to leave. But soldiers took hold of him and locked him up in a blockhouse where he was held so long that his son Ellimpsico and another friendly chieftain, Red Hawk, grew alarmed for his safety. Knowing where he had gone, they went after him. They too were confined in the makeshift jail.

A day or so afterward a few Kentucky militiamen from the stockade rowed to the north shore of the Ohio on a foraging party and there got into a scrape with a stray band of Indians. One of the men, whose name was Gilmore, was shot in the scuffle, which put the others of the garrison into such a fury that they entered

SIMON BECOMES MOROSE

the blockhouse and with knife and tomahawk butchered Cornstalk, Red Hawk and the youth Ellimpsico.

With such bloody remembrances to stir a tribe of warriors noted for their pursuit of vengeance and for the stoicism with which they accepted death, the work of the British Indian Agents at Detroit became a simple matter. And doubtless Girty and those other men sent out by Hamilton to lead the aborigines often found themselves following instead of being to the fore.

Still another occurrence which quickened the braves of the Ohio country that year was the council of the Seneca-Iroquois confederacy called by the sachems of those eastern tribes to decide what would be their stand during the Revolution. For the Senecas not only declared themselves for war upon the United States, they also ordered the Delawares to join them.

This split the Delaware tribe. About half of the braves sided with Captain Pipe, which name translated back into his own tongue was Hopocan. He was a Delaware chieftain who had already journeyed to Detroit and had taken the war hatchet handed him by Hamilton. But others, particularly those close to the Moravian Missions at Salem, Schönbrunn and Gnadenhutten, remained steadfast and nodded assent to the indignant speech of Chief White Eyes, who thus bawled out his challenge to the Senecas:

THE WHITE SAVAGE

"White Eyes knows well that the Senecas consider the Delaware a conquered tribe—as women—as their inferiors. They have—say they—shortened the Delaware's legs and put petticoats on us. They say they have given us a hoe with a cornpounder and told us to pound and plant for them—those men—those warriors! But look at White Eyes! Is he not full grown? Wears he not a warrior's dress? Ai, he is a man—and these are the arms of a man—and all this land belongs to the Delawares."

Chief White Eyes and his men about those Moravian missions along the Muskingum were the one great snag in the course of the Detroit British Indian Agents voyaging about the Ohio country. They were established within the Indian domain, but near enough to Fort Pitt for intelligence of English or native war movements to be conveyed there, often in time for the Americans to prepare for these intended surprises. Hamilton had tried to bribe these Delawares, had threatened them, but had got nowhere with them. For when White Eyes' tribe finally agreed to go to war it was at the request of the Americans and on the side of the Americans, to whom, at a council on the Muskingum, they promised to furnish a considerable number of warriors to fight the British.

So in this long-distance and rather ineffectual duel

SIMON BECOMES MOROSE

between Detroit and Fort Pitt the Indians were of advantage to both the British and Americans—to almost everybody but themselves. But those who joined the United States jeopardized their race to the greatest extent. For with the Delawares under White Eyes amiable to the Pennsylvanians the commandant at Fort Pitt—where General McIntosh had replaced General Hand—was enabled to build forts in the Ohio wilderness. One of these, Fort McIntosh, was on the right bank of the Ohio River; the other, Fort Laurens, was seventy miles through the forests towards the Tuscarawas.

It was through the erection of these two forts that Simon Girty reappears again in the border annals. He had left Kenton in the late fall of 1778. Within a month he had received orders from General Hamilton to reconnoiter the country between the Tuscarawas and Ohio rivers. Hamilton had received vague reports of American activities in that vicinity and, anticipating an attack upon Detroit, he wanted more direct information with regard to them. In January, with seventeen Shawanese braves, Girty left the Scioto and set out through the snowy wilderness.

Girty had known of the existence of Fort Laurens before he left the Scioto. He did not know the fort by name, but he had heard that one was there. That was all he did know. As to the officer in charge—it happened to be Colonel John Gibson, the man who copied Logan's speech for Girty—, the size of the garrison, the exact position of the fort and the strength of its walls, those were pieces of information which he had to discover so that he could report them to General Hamilton. Hence the capture of a few of Gibson's men would be valuable.

The way in which Girty proposed to take these captives, if Brother David Zeisberger, one of the Moravian missionaries with Brother John Heckenwelder, is to be believed, was as follows: He had discovered that the Delawares allied with the Americans surmounted their headdress with deers' tails so as to be distinguished from passive or enemy Indians in that neighborhood and he planned that by the use of these tails on his own braves he would be permitted to pass into the fort without being suspected and so would find means of taking one or two of Gibson's men with him. He also, if there is any truth in Zeisberger, had designs on Gibson's scalp, and on the journey was loudly threatening.

That Girty, when he reached the Delawares, boasted he would take the scalp of the officer in charge of Fort Laurens is probable enough. But that he mentioned this officer by name (which one of his biographers states and which is to be inferred from a letter written by Zeis-

SIMON BECOMES MOROSE

berger) is hard to believe. For how was he to know that Gibson was in command unless some Delaware had told him; and how was this Delaware, to whom as to all Indians the titles of white men were a mystery, to say "Colonel John Gibson" to Girty?

But at any rate Girty or some of his associates talked too much and in a wrong quarter for their object to remain a secret. Killbuck, a Delaware chief in Coshocton, heard Girty's plans announced and straightway sent a runner to Zeisberger at the Moravian Missions up the river. And Zeisberger hastily forwarded the information to Colonel Gibson that Simon Girty and twenty-five warriors were on their way to Fort Laurens and planned to bring back the commandant's scalp.

That message from Zeisberger put Girty's reconnoitering party on a personal basis, made it appear as a challenge to a duel between Girty and Colonel Gibson. For Gibson, naturally resentful and infuriated when he received word of the threat, entered into the man-to-man phase of it very quickly. And in letters—which never reached their intended destination—he declared that he not only hoped to prevent his former acquaintance from taking his scalp, but that he thought he should be "able to trepan him" instead.

Girty made no attempt to enter Fort Laurens, neither by force nor by the fictitious strategy of the deers' tails.

THE WHITE SAVAGE

On the contrary, he took his braves along the trail that led from Laurens to McIntosh and halted them for an ambush. That, it is likely, had been his plan from the beginning. However, there the warriors, subsisting on a few handfuls of parched corn a day, waited in the January weather. And after a while Captain John Clark of the Eighth Pennsylvania Regiment, who had taken a load of supplies from Fort Pitt to Gibson and whose tracks Girty had doubtless discovered, passed by on his return with fourteen privates and a sergeant.

As it was now well known that a band of warriors under Girty was somewhere within the seventy miles between Forts Laurens and McIntosh, only carelessness on the part of Gibson would have permitted a force so small to make the return journey. A few more squads would not have appreciably weakened his garrison; they might have saved the escort from losing in the encounter that followed.

Nevertheless Clark was allowed to leave the fort not only with an insufficient number, but also to carry letters with which Gibson had entrusted one of Clark's men—letters which if intercepted by Girty would be of value to General Hamilton at Detroit.

Clark and his men left Fort Laurens. They had got about three miles outside of the gates when the wood and underbrush through which they were passing grew

SIMON BECOMES MOROSE

loud with warriors' yells and the burst and rattle of musketry. Some of the escort fell. Those that remained standing, if they returned the Indians' fire at all, were assailed by Girty and his braves before they had a chance to reload their clumsy muskets. With two men of Clark's party killed and four of them wounded it was a foot race for the rest. Clark, his sergeant, and seven privates beat their way back into the fort and the gates were closed behind them, but one who had kept his legs was overtaken by the Indians and bound.

Among those of Clark's convoy who did not safely return to the fort was the man whom Colonel Gibson had entrusted with the letters. Girty discovered the packet. One of them contained the important news that General McIntosh was planning to move with an army from Fort Pitt to attack Detroit some time in the following March. But what interested him most were the words in Colonel Gibson's hand, the words staring up at him, "I hope, if Mr. Girty comes to pay me a visit, I shall be able to trepan him." So then, it was Gibson who commanded at Fort Laurens! And Gibson had been informed that he, Girty, was to be in that vicinity. Not only that, but had hoped—what did the letter say? —"hope I shall be able to trepan him." God damn. First there had come the shock of his meeting with Kenton. And now old Gibson was wanting to take his scalp!

THE WHITE SAVAGE

He hadn't bargained for this kind of thing when he ran away from Fort Pitt.

With his prisoner and the information he had gathered, Girty set out for Detroit, but stopped at Coshocton among some Delawares and at Upper Sandusky among the Wyandots. Both towns were on the main trail. In spite of the success of his enterprise he was dispirited. For Gibson's words kept clanking ominously against his ears. He was surprised, bewildered, and felt as though everywhere along the border frontiersmen were vindictively waiting to settle a special account with a man called Girty.

As Girty admitted to Kenton the one time he saw him in the wilderness he had been too hasty in absconding from Fort Pitt. He might have added that had it not been for chance placing him in the way of Alexander McKee he would never have attempted to make the journey from the Ohio through the Indian country to General Hamilton at Detroit. But even after he did leave he must not have felt that he was committing the unforgivable crime of treason. He could only have told himself that he was departing from a place where he was held to be of small account (else why, with all his experience, he might have argued, was he given a mere second-lieutenancy?) and going where he might expect more appreciation; that a man's first business is to help

[100]

SIMON BECOMES MOROSE

himself; that he was injuring nobody in particular. Perhaps he thought even less than that as he left Fort Pitt; at any rate only a maniac—which he was far from being—would have deserted with the intention of returning to kill and plunder.

Gibson's threat against him was still in Girty's mind when he came back to the Delaware country four months later. He had taken his prisoner to Detroit, where Captain Lernoult—temporarily in command while Hamilton, who had led a force against Vincennes and had been beaten by George Rogers Clark, was journeying up the Ohio in chains—welcomed him. Girty had been able to inform Lernoult that Forts McIntosh and Laurens had been erected in the Ohio wilderness, that the General at Fort Pitt intended moving against Detroit in March and that a host of Indians, particularly Wyandots and those stray Senecas known as Mingoes, were ready to take to the warpath against these invading Americans and only awaited supplies and somebody to lead them.

During those four months Lernoult had sent out a party of Indians under Captain Henry Bird. They laid long siege to Fort Laurens, but at last had to give up. And General McIntosh had not only dropped his plans for a march to Detroit; he had relinquished his post as commandant at Fort Pitt as well. As for Girty he had made a daring trip into the neighborhood of Fort Pitt in order to secure some papers which a disaffected American there had written and had hidden in a hollow tree for the perusal of the British.

It was July of 1779 when Girty reappeared at Coshocton. He had the papers which he had been sent for, but he was morose, looking at Heckewelder and Zeisberger with an angry, suspicious eye, exploding to Richard Connor, an American trader who had stopped there, that, by God, he didn't expect the Americans to show any favors to him, neither would he show any to them!

Lean, sallow Heckewelder was at hand to hear these words repeated and in the next of his chain of innumerable letters to the authorities at Fort Pitt he reported them. From the beginning of the War of the Revolution until the end Heckewelder, as long as he was able, continued to send messengers to Pittsburgh with every scrap of news that related to British and Indian movements in that part of the country. Which was, of course, his own affair. But while his active sympathy thus expressed gave the various commandants at Fort Pitt opportunities to ward off British and Indian attacks, he might have realized that in taking up his self-appointed position as informer he was endangering the Delawares' lives even while trying to save their souls.

SIMON BECOMES MOROSE

Whenever those two met—the long, thin, dour Heckewelder and the solid, round-eyed Girty, both of whom were about the same age—Heckewelder always said a few prayers. For he suspected, in his ingenious way, that Simon was about to kill him. That was nonsense, as any less fearful man would have known. But there is this much to be said about it: within a little more than a year after Girty reported at Detroit he became an ardent worker towards British ends. And as such he was aware that not only Heckewelder but all of the Moravian missionaries about the Muskingum were an obstruction and it would be better if they were removed. But General Hamilton, always considerate of the missionaries if towards nobody else, refused to have them disturbed. So Girty could do nothing. He once glared at Brother David Zeisberger and remarked that he wished the whole damned mission was in his power; which quickly aroused Heckewelder to write Colonel Brodhead, then commandant at Fort Pitt, that Girty had tried to kill his fellow cure of aboriginal souls.

It was this frequent mention of Girty's name in letters written by Heckewelder that was largely responsible for the borderers' belief that every evening at sundown Girty poised with a horde of screaming warriors on the east bank of the Ohio preparatory to a murderous foray on some lonely cabin. In that summer of 1779 when

THE WHITE SAVAGE

Simon went after the packet of papers already referred to he heard the further disturbing news that Pennsylvania had offered a reward of eight hundred dollars for his head.

That Girty had no liking for Heckewelder or for those Delawares about Coshocton, or that he grew more desperate in his marauds is scarcely to be wondered at. For many of the Delawares, inspired by the vision of all the barrels of rum they could buy for eight hundred dollars, leered at him in a peculiarly lean and thirsty fashion; naturally, increasing hate on one side increases it on the other.

A letter, either written by him or for him at that time, shows not only his feeling for the Coshocton Delawares, but also gives evidence of his deepening connections with the Indians. It was sent to Captain Lernoult, still in command at Detroit, on September 6, 1779, by messenger from Sandusky, where there was a British trading post.

Girty wrote: "Sir, I take the liberty to acquaint you that I intend leaving this place tomorrow. There is a party of twenty-five Wyandots that have been turned to go as volunteers with me on the road I proposed when leaving Detroit: likewise a party of ten Mingoes, which party Sandithtas commands. The Wyandots are commanded by Seyatamah.

SIMON BECOMES MOROSE

"Sir, I refer you to Captain [Alexander] McKee for the knowledge of the above-mentioned chiefs, if you are not already acquainted with their names. Tomorrow, my friend Nouthsaka sets off with ten warriors for the Falls of the Ohio. Our great friend, Captain Pipe [Hopocan] is gone to Fort Pitt to a council; likewise Maulmatas and Duentate. Six days ago a party of Wyandots brought here three prisoners from Kentucky. They say there are three hundred men under pay [militiamen] in those parts. They also say there are nine forts in and about Kentucky.

"There are certain accounts of the rebels leaving Tuscarawas [Fort Laurens]. I intend to go there directly and shall send you the token you gave me at Detroit if they are not there. If the Delawares are in possession of the fort, I intend to turn them out and burn the fort (if my party are able), as you gave me the liberty to act as I thought best, and they and I are not on the best of terms.

"Yesterday Sandithtas arrived here with the account of ten parties of Shawanese that are gone to war. This is all I have to acquaint you with at present."

Girty was, and had been considered before this, a trusted and valuable man in the British Indian Department. The spring before, Captain Bird had affirmed to Lernoult, "Girty, I assure you, sir, is one of the most useful, disinterested friends in his department that the government has." And now, a few weeks after Girty dispatched the above letter, he was to show himself to be as doughty at fighting men armed and prepared as he had been in marauding scantily protected settlements and making ambushes for unwary escorts.

In the early part of October, 1779, Girty was close to the Ohio River with his brother George, Matthew Elliott and nearly a hundred Indians under his command. They were mostly Shawanese, Wyandots and Delawares and all of them were ready to fight, else they would not have gathered in so large a number on the southern edge of their country. Whether or not they knew it at the time, a force of about seventy Americans under David Rogers was moving up the Ohio River. They were coming in keelboats in which they guarded a great supply of military stores for Virginia troops.

Rogers had made a long journey—from New Orleans, where he had bought clothing, rum, fusees and other goods for the Virginians. Most of his trip was passed without mishap, but when he got between the mouths of the Little Miami, on the north side, and the Licking on the south, he discovered Indians ahead. It was on October 4. Quickly he landed on the Kentucky bank and began drawing the keelboats to the shore. His men clambered out and deployed through the woods in

SIMON BECOMES MOROSE

the Indian fashion, hoping to come upon and surprise the band of braves which they had sighted.

It was in the morning and half of the hundred braves under Girty and Elliott had not yet returned from hunting when the news was brought to Simon that a party of Long Knives was approaching. He too was on the Kentucky side and Rogers' men were moving directly towards him.

Doubtless underestimating the size of the white force (as Rogers unquestionably underestimated the strength of the savages), Girty called out the Indian cry for the attack and the braves went speeding among the trees through which the enemy were coming upon them. They met, fought hard and hand to hand, with Girty well to the forefront of the braves.

The meeting must have been short but terrific. Of Rogers' men not less than forty-two were killed, the commander among them. Girty's warriors suffered the loss of two men mortally fallen and three with gunshot wounds that were not serious.

The supplies that had been intended for the Virginia troops were taken by the victors, who had discovered the well-stored keelboats farther down the river. And likely enough there was that night on the Ohio shore a drinking party in which Simon again distinguished himself.

THE WHITE SAVAGE

Now Girty was giving the Pennsylvanians and Virginians some good cause to offer a reward for his head, to single him out from all of the disaffected borderers (there were perhaps more than a hundred) who left the United States either to travel the wilderness directly to Detroit or to remain with one of the Indian tribes. In the spring of the following year, which was 1780, he was again in the Kentucky country, not in command this time, but as an interpreter and guide. Captain Henry Bird was in charge of the expedition and had set out from Detroit with more than a hundred and fifty Canadians, a hundred Indians from the regions of the lakes, and two small howitzers. He made the journey downward by raft and pirogue, taking the Maumee from Lake Erie to the St. Joseph portage, then down the Great Miami and along the Ohio. On the Miami Alexander McKee, risen by that time to the post of deputy Indian Agent, had joined him with reinforcements that more than doubled his command. The comparatively large and well-equipped body then went up the Ohio to the Licking and up the Licking between Kentucky banks.

Aiming at Ruddle's station, Alexander McKee was sent ahead with two hundred warriors while Captain Bird and the rest followed more slowly. McKee came within sight of the log-built fort in the evening and by nightfall had placed his Indians so as to encircle it.

SIMON BECOMES MOROSE

When dawn came the braves immediately set up a brisk firing at chinks between the logs and at the loopholes in the blockhouses. Throughout the morning their musketry was answered from within, but at noon Captain Bird arrived with his main force and unloaded one of their cannon from the pirogue which they had poled up the river. The weapon was put into position, trained on the stockade. It roared out shot which ripped through the logs, splintering a wide hole. Captain Bird turned to Girty and sent him with a white flag across the clearing to demand immediate surrender.

Girty stepped forth with the flag above his head. The firing ceased. He walked on, crossing the stump-cluttered ground to the pickets, whom he coolly informed (one of his biographers states that he was cool, but it is likely he blustered a little to hide his nervousness) that if they didn't give up at once they would all be killed.

This ultimatum he also spoke to Isaac Ruddle, but Ruddle wanted terms before he would agree to let down the bars that held the gates fast. He asked that his men and their families be put under the protection of the British and saved from the torture of the Indians.

Girty retired, taking this information to Captain Bird to consider. And Bird, though he should have known better, for he had experience in trying to curb battle-warmed savages, consented that the captives should be guarded by his own white men. Further resistance being useless, the gates were then swung open.

But as soon as the bars were withdrawn the Indians rushed into the stockade with knife and tomahawk. In Bird's own sad words they "tore the poor children from their mothers' breasts, killed and wounded many." They spared nothing and acted not only with the greatest cruelty but were so maddened that they destroyed a herd of cattle which would otherwise have kept them from half starving on their way back north.

Bird managed, however, to retrieve a number of the prisoners. These he carefully guarded. But his expedition was near its end. After one more assault the men had to turn back for lack of provisions, and the capture of Louisville, which he had had in mind, was abandoned.

Girty followed the army back across the Ohio, but then struck off towards his cabin at Solomon's town to be among the Mingoes again. There he began to hear of events that were taking place among the Delawares and Moravian Mission Indians in the neighborhood of Coshocton. He might have learned that Brother John Gottlieb Ernestus Heckewelder had been married to Miss Sarah Ohneburg, a teacher in his mission . . . he did hear the more interesting news that the United States

SIMON BECOMES MOROSE

government, pinched for money and supplies, was not carrying out its part of the treaty which it had made with the Coshocton Delawares and that in consequence these Indians were beginning to mutter that they had been deceived. The war chief Wingenund and other Delaware leaders between the Muskingum and the Tuscarawas were thinking of breaking their alliance with America and forming another with England.

*Those Damned Missionaries; and the Butchering and
Burning of Their Hapless Brood*

CHAPTER VI

Those Damned Missionaries; and the Butchering and Burning of their Hapless Brood

WHEN Chatham, protesting to the British parliament against his country's authorized use of the Indians in the War of the Revolution, spoke of it as "letting loose the horrible hell-hounds of savage war" he gave the British Indian Department credit for more power than it possessed. For no man in Canada had ever held the Indians in check, so they couldn't very well be let loose. The Ohio Indians, with that patriotic ardor which people praise when it acts towards their good and condemn when it affects them unfavorably, simply fought to hold back the frontier and to repay in kind the murder of members of their families. Thus, it must be repeated, the aims of the aborigines and those of the people of the United States were directly opposed and an Indian war could scarcely have been avoided. But as for England, whose colonization schemes had been halted by the revolution, she had no such difficulties. No settlers came into the Ohio country under the British flag, only traders who wanted furs and were willing to be agreeable to the Indians in order to get them.

It seems more natural than fiendish, then, that the Delawares about Coshocton should have become hostile to the borderers again when the Federal government failed to preserve its share of the treaty. During the fall of 1780 Wingenund and other chieftains prepared to turn against the frontier. In the following winter they sent a message to Major De Peyster, then commandant at Detroit, asking that friendly relations be reestablished between themselves and Britain.

The Christianized Delawares, however, remained amiable towards the United States. There were several hundred of them in the three mission villages on the Tuscarawas and it was with pride and self-congratulation that their spiritual father, Heckewelder, looked on their sheeplike devotion. But for the Delawares who had not been baptized he had no such fondness. And it made him bitter to hear that they were denouncing the United States government. His imagination vaulted above the facts of the case and he wrote Colonel Brodhead that these Delawares were planning a war party against the border. He hoped, he added, that if Wingenund and his braves did attack the Americans the Delawares would be properly beaten.

As far as the Delawares' change of feeling is concerned Heckewelder reported truly, but whether they had actually struck the war pole may be doubted. For even after the missionary had informed Brodhead that "the greater part of them (the warriors) will be upon you in a few days," they had gone no further than to forward a speech to Detroit, by way of Half King, a Wyandot chief at Sandusky, asking that Major De Peyster send traders—not soldiers—among them and telling him that as they had been deceived by the Americans they would listen to them no longer. No act of aggression was mentioned in the message; which would certainly have been done had they had any definite plans against the border at that time. For in facing about from Americans to British and seeking the latter's support they would have endeavored to prove the earnestness of their decision by whatever means they had at hand.

Nevertheless Brodhead, on receiving Heckewelder's report, began to make ready for an expedition against the Indians about Coshocton, exclusive, of course, of those Delawares in the Moravian missions whom Heckewelder, Zeisberger, Post and Bull had converted to Christianity.

Meanwhile Girty had gone to Detroit where, on the twelfth of April, two days after Brodhead had crossed the Ohio with three hundred men, he sponsored

THE WHITE SAVAGE

the following message which Major De Peyster wrote in his name to the Delawares:

"Indians of Coshocton! I have received your speech sent me by the Half King of Sandusky. It contains three strings, one of them white and the other two checkered. You say that you want traders to be sent to your villages and that you are resolved no more to listen to the Virginians [all Americans, that is], who have deceived you. It would give me pleasure again to receive you as brothers, both for your own good and for the friendship I bear to the Indians in general." After Girty's name had been signed to this message he went to Half King's village on the Sandusky, where he waited, expecting that a closer alliance with the Delawares would follow.

Girty had barely arrived at Upper Sandusky when Colonel Brodhead came within sight of Coshocton, or rather Salem, the lower Moravian settlement on the Tuscarawas. There, on April 20, which was a dark, chilly day, the colonel halted his troops and waited for one of his runners whom he had sent after Brother John Heckewelder. The runner returned with the missionary (who left his wife and daughter Mary, born just four days earlier) and a supply of dried corn and meat from the Indians' store. Brodhead's outfit ate the provisions and then, after mutual expressions of good will, the two men parted. Brodhead led his army towards Coshocton, which he had so closely approached without raising an alarm.

But on his way along the east bank of the river Brodhead's scouts discovered Indians. The scouts fired, though not well enough to prevent two of the Delawares from escaping. Now it was essential that Brodhead reach Coshocton almost on the heels of the fleeing braves, else none would be there for him to kill when he arrived. His troops broke into a run, were undeterred by a heavy and unexpected rain. They arrived at Coshocton and took the town without a shot having been fired. There women, children and braves were herded together. Fifteen of the latter were killed with spears and tomahawks, then scalped.

As night came on Brodhead pitched his camp and a guard of regulars was placed over the prisoners. The soldiers settled down to sleep and sentries were posted to watch the west bank of the river for any hostile demonstration from Delawares in the village on that side which Brodhead had been unable to reach on account of the high water that lay flush with the stream's banks. The night passed quietly.

At dawn a Delaware chieftain stood on the west shore and halloed across the water, saying that he had word for the white captain.

Brodhead himself shouted back for him to speak. Thus encouraged, the Indian answered, "Peace!"

"If you want peace send over some of your chiefs!" answered Brodhead.

But the Indian was suspicious of this. "Maybe you kill!" he said uneasily.

He was answered, "They shall not be killed."

With this assurance one of the chieftains, an agreeable looking man, appeared and crossed over in a canoe. Brodhead met him as he alighted on the bank and they began to talk.

While the two men stood there one of the Wetzels (either Jacob or Lewis was capable of what followed) stepped noiselessly up behind the chieftain. Wetzel had a tomahawk lying against his breast beneath his hunting jacket. Suddenly the tomahawk flashed outward and up, then down. The blade went into the back of the chieftain's skull and he fell dead.

That ended the peace parley.

At noon Brodhead began his march back towards Fort Pitt. His prisoners were under the charge of some militiamen. Half a mile from Coshocton they found their charges had become a nuisance. They began murdering them.

A further account of Brodhead's capture of Coshocton is given by Girty from a party of twenty Wyandots

THOSE DAMNED MISSIONARIES

whom he had sent there but who had not arrived until after the American colonel's departure. Immediately he had a letter written to De Peyster in which he gave the news that they had brought:

" . . . Colonel Brodhead, with five hundred men [Dodderidge gives the number at eight hundred and Butterfield at three hundred], burned the town and killed fifteen men. He left six houses on this [the west] side of the creek that he did not see. He likewise took the women and children prisoners, but afterwards let them go. He let four men go that were prisoners who showed him a paper that they had from Congress. Brodhead told them that it was none of his fault that their people were killed, but the fault of the militia that would not be under his command [they would not obey, that is]. He likewise told them that in seven months he would beat all of the Indians out of the country. In six days from this date he is to set off for this place with one thousand men; and Colonel [George Rogers] Clark is gone down the Ohio with one thousand men.

"There were one hundred and twenty Wyandots ready to start off with me until this news came. Your children will be very glad if you will send these people you promised to send to their assistance; likewise send the Indians that are about you to assist us. The Christian Indians have applied to us to move them off before the rebels come to their town, etc. . . ."

As Girty's letter suggests—shows plainly, it might be said,—the tempo of action was increasing in the Ohio country. Colonel Brodhead's advance upon his former allies at Coshocton had, quite naturally, turned nearly all of the Delawares against him. And his threat that within a week he was to come again and, with a thousand men, complete the destruction he had begun, whipped up their fear. As for Girty he stood fast in the face of this, waiting at Upper Sandusky for volunteers from Detroit. Yet he was well aware that De Peyster would be unable to send him enough reinforcements to compete against the thousand militiamen of which Brodhead had boasted. He also knew what would be his fate if he were taken by the Americans: some time earlier Pennsylvania had adjudged himself, Alexander McKee and Matthew Elliott as traitors. There was also the eight hundred dollars' reward on his head. Nevertheless he remained where he was, which was no more than twenty miles from Coshocton.

But those thousand men that Colonel Brodhead was to muster against Sandusky never materialized. And before the seven months had passed—in seven months he had said that all of the Indians would have been driven out of the Ohio country—he had been relieved as the commandant at Fort Pitt by Colonel John Gibson, who, by November, was replaced by Brigadier General William Irvine. As for the report that Colonel George Rogers Clark was marching an army against the Ohio country, it was true: he aimed in a roundabout way at Detroit.

Within two weeks after Girty had asked Major De Peyster for troops to repel the anticipated attack of Colonel Brodhead, there were brought before the Wyandot council at Sandusky ten white male prisoners from the Virginia and Kentucky borders. They had been taken by marauding Indians who had watched the tide of spring immigration flow down between the Ohio's thickly wooded banks. One of the ten was an eighteen-year-old youth named Henry Baker, who had been captured at Wheeling Creek. At the Wyandot council he and nine others were forced to run the gauntlet. Then they were led into the council house and condemned to be burned at the stake, one each day until they all were dead. Young Baker, who was to be the last, saw nine fateful dawns and nine miserable nights; and finally, on the tenth day, braves came into the tent where he was lying, and unfastened the thongs that bound him. With a brave on either side of him they led him forth to the charred stake.

Young Baker had made no resistance as the braves

THE WHITE SAVAGE

took him towards the stake, but when he was within a few steps of the place of doom he balked with all his energy. For he saw a white rider on a swift horse coming up the trail from the wilderness. He held back, tried to jerk his arms from the grip of his captors, pleaded and argued with them, trying to gain a few moments. But the braves drew him on towards the faggots which had been piled in a circle about the stake. Baker screamed and gave a final wrench, his head turned imploringly towards the white horseman.

The rider was Girty, who stopped. He looked down at young Baker and asked him a question. Held by the braves, Baker faced away from the dreaded stake and came nearer Girty, telling him his name and where he had been captured.

By this time several Indians had gathered and there were chiefs among them. To these men Girty spoke, asking that the youth be spared, though doubtless giving as his reason the fact that Baker was worth more to them alive than dead.

There was a short conference among the chiefs. Meanwhile Girty talked to the boy, asking him questions concerning the neighborhood of Wheeling. These Baker answered and had the vain hope that if he were freed the white man meant to send him back to his people. Then the chiefs returned and gave word that they had agreed to Girty's request and that the white youth was to be saved; and soon afterward Baker was sent to Detroit, where Major De Peyster released him.

Granted that Girty did nothing extraordinary in interceding for Henry Baker. Nevertheless it was an act that should be remembered to his sorely needed credit. For a year later he was to stand in a shadow so dark and cast by so lurid a light that his former countrymen, in later referring to the scene, have vilified him as being among the lowest specimens humanity has ever offered. It should also be kept in mind that the Wyandots were his friends, which greatly increased the possibility of their granting him such a favor; that when they had led Baker to the stake their blood was not heated by personal revenge, and that the youth, if spared, might have given them valuable information. None of these circumstances were present at the scene already referred to which Girty took part in a year after Baker had been released.

While Simon was spending that spring at Upper Sandusky his brother George and Captain Andrew Brant (Theyandenegea, the Mohawk chieftain) were lying hidden along the banks of the Ohio, where they were waiting for Colonel Lochry and his detachment, which were bound for Louisville to join the force of George Rogers Clark. George Girty had had a curious life since leaving Fort Pitt. Personal affairs had taken him to St. Louis and there he had been shanghaied and forced into the service of Captain Willing's company of freshwater Marines. Even in those days, it appears, Marines had a way of being hard-boiled. But though George had been given a lieutenancy it had not contented him. He deserted and after a long journey reached Detroit, where he entered the British Indian service. A competent man with gun and tomahawk, he was assisted by another who was equally capable—Theyandenegea, or Captain Brant.

One day while George Girty, Brant and the braves lay in ambush along the Ohio they saw Colonel Archibald Lochry and his hundred Pennsylvanians coming down the river. They sprang out at once and made a complete surprise. Most of Lochry's men were killed outright, but a few, among whom was seventeen-year-old Christian Fast, were taken prisoners. So complete was their victory that they were exceptionally well pleased with themselves. Carrying their booty of scalps, rum and provisions, they swaggered down the Ohio, then up the Great Miami where they were to meet a force of British and Indians who were coming from Detroit to attack Clark's main army at Louisville.

The command of this expedition from Detroit was divided between Captain Thompson, who had the Canadian rangers, and Alexander McKee, who was to lead

Theyandenegea (Captain Brant), from a mezzotint after Romney's portrait

the Indians. McKee had picked up Simon Girty as he passed southward and Simon accompanied them to the Great Miami, where the Indians under his brother George and Captain Brant were added to the company. From the Great Miami the whole body proceeded towards Louisville, where Clark was then encamped.

It was during the dull, irritating days of waiting on the north bank of the Ohio that Brant, having drunk too much that night, began glorifying himself as a mighty man of war and telling of his deeds against the dead Lochry and his soldiers. Whereupon Simon, likewise drunk, frankly sneered. A little later he was calling Theyandenegea a liar.

But this was too much for the Indian's pride. In a fury he dropped his hand to his sword hilt and whirled the blade at Simon's skull, then looked dazedly at the stream of blood which flowed down Girty's round face and matted his coarse black hair.

It was the one blow struck. It stretched Simon out and he had to be carried by his heels and shoulders to his tent. In the weeks before he was able to rise of his own accord Captain Thompson and McKee discovered that Clark had given up his movement against Detroit, making it no longer necessary for them to interpose the Indians and the rangers between him and his goal.

In the meantime a scene had been enacted at the

THE WHITE SAVAGE

Moravian missions which doubtless pleased Simon enormously when he heard of it, but which, as a step leading to the greater spectacle that was to make his memory abhorred by the generation that came after him, he might not have liked so well. It began in this way.

Matthew Elliott, who had been promoted to a captaincy in the British Indian service, marched from Sandusky in late August with a party of savages and French-Canadians to the Tuscarawas and the Moravian missions. After a skirmish eastward they entered the Moravian villages and demanded that Heckewelder, the other missionaries, and the Christianized Delawares as well, leave their cabins at once and accompany them back to the Sandusky. In this Elliott had two motives. The first was to get Heckewelder and Zeisberger farther away from the border so that they would be less able to keep up their correspondence with the American authorities at Fort Pitt. The other was to remove the converted Delawares to a place of greater safety. The Delawares themselves had requested it, for another expedition was being aimed at them by the militiamen of Pennsylvania.

Protesting angrily but without success, Heckewelder, Zeisberger and their families both real and spiritual were taken westward from the Tuscarawas and settled on a stretch of land not far from Upper Sandusky.

In ordering the removal of these Christianized Dela-

THOSE DAMNED MISSIONARIES

wares Matthew Elliott had stood for no delay. Consequently the fields of corn which they had planted about Salem, Gnadenhutten and Schönbrunn earlier in the year remained standing with the ears still in the husks. After Elliott had taken them to their new and less pleasant home they often looked back longingly towards those former villages of theirs which really seemed to be Tents of Grace and Beautiful Spring. They remembered the unhusked corn and the warmth of their cabins.

For there was nothing beautiful or comfortable about Upper Sandusky. The land was sandy, the trees scraggly, and the marshes dreary. In their new abode they lived in tiny huts in which only the scantiest fires could be made; there were no floors and scarcely any timber to keep them warm throughout the approaching winter. The pasture, too, was lean and their few heads of cattle became like skeletons and gave little milk.

But even so they were in no worse shape than the Wyandots among whom they lived, not even the chieftains and Simon Girty. Girty had recovered from his wound and had returned to Upper Sandusky in the fall. As winter shut down the daily rations of the Christianized Delawares near him were reduced to a pint of corn for each person. "Yet," wrote Heckewelder later, "in this wretched situation, the hungry Wyandots would often come to our huts to see if there was any victuals cooking, or ready cooked. At one time, just as my wife had set down to what was intended for our dinner, the Half King, Simon Girty and another, a Wyandot, entered my cabin, and seeing the victuals ready, without ceremony, began eating."

Or were affairs so bad that winter of 1781-82 as Heckewelder afterward made out? For he also says that Alexander McCormick, a British trader at Upper Sandusky, now and again sent him a leg of venison which McCormick had bought from one of the hunters; and if venison was to be had for the shooting it is unlikely that Girty was so ravenous when he and the Half King began eating Heckewelder's meal, but rather that it was his uncouth way of plaguing the missionary.

But Heckewelder's obtuseness was proof against his understanding of even such simple human frailties. It was incomprehensible to him that Girty and the Half King should be angered because he acted as an informer to the authorities at Pittsburgh; that they should be eager to get him and the rest of the missionaries out of the country.

Earlier, before Elliott broke up the missions, Half King had appealed to the Christianized Delawares themselves. He had said to them, "Cousins, you Indians in Gnadenhutten, Schönbrunn and Salem who believe in the Long Knives' God! Half King is much concerned

THOSE DAMNED MISSIONARIES

on your account, because you live in a dangerous locality. Two powerful, merciless and angry tribes, the English and the Long Knives, stand ready, opening their jaws against each other like monstrous beasts. You are sitting down between both of them and are in danger of being devoured and ground to powder, if not in the jaws of one, then in the jaws of the other, or even both.

"Consider your own people! Consider your wives and children and preserve their lives from these crouching monsters. For here they all must perish. Half King therefore takes you by the hand, lifts you up and places you in the care of the white captain (Major De Peyster) where you will be safe. Do not stand looking at your plantations, but arise and follow Half King; take also your white priests with you and worship the Great Spirit as you have been accustomed to, only in the place to which Half King shall lead you. This is Half King's message and he has come solely for the purpose of delivering it."

It was excellent advice. But the converted Delawares had sat lymphatic, trusting to Heckewelder and Zeisberger who were so wise about the Great Spirit that controlled all things. They had moved only when there was a force behind them. And now they huddled in their tiny, smoke-filled cabins through the long winter of the desolate Wyandot country of Upper Sandusky.

THE WHITE SAVAGE

Helpless themselves, they looked for support towards Heckewelder and the other missionaries, who were equally helpless. Since their removal it was as though the skies had darkened above them and as if that darkness followed wherever they went.

In the midst of the cold winter plans were being made by which these dazedly moving people should lose even the little support which they had come to depend on. Girty and the Half King felt that the Wyandot country was not far enough away from Fort Pitt to prevent Heckewelder and Zeisberger from continuing their correspondence with General Irvine. They wanted these missionaries entirely out of the Ohio country. So Girty had a letter written for the Half King to Major De Peyster which stated that the Wyandot warriors would remain uneasy and in fear of betrayal so long as Zeisberger and Heckewelder remained in the neighborhood.

It was while this letter was traveling by runner from Sandusky to Detroit that a great many of the Christianized Indians, having scarcely any provisions left, were permitted to go back through the snowy wilderness to gather the corn that stood about the towns of peaceful-sounding names from which they had been taken. They departed in small groups, some as early as January 16 and some not until the ninth of February. They made

THOSE DAMNED MISSIONARIES

it a family party by taking their wives and children. But none of their white mentors went along.

By the latter part of February all of them had arrived at their former homes. There they began to husk the corn. Each day they stacked their arms and went into the white bottomlands of the Tuscarawas to jerk the ears from the frozen stalks. They worked slowly and many nights were spent in their cabins. But by the sixth of March, though most of the corn had been gathered, from Schönbrunn down through Gnadenhutten to Salem on the bend of the river these Christianized families were still laboring in the fields.

On the night before, a force of Fort Pitt militiamen commanded by Colonel David Williamson arrived within a mile of Gnadenhutten and pitched their camp. They numbered an even hundred and had come as avengers of several borderers who had been killed that month by marauding Indians. Precisely where they intended going would be hard to determine. For a body so small would never have dared attack the Sandusky towns and the only other villages between these and Fort Pitt were at Coshocton. But that they had Coshocton for their objective is equally doubtful, for they must have known that the Indians had removed farther into the wilderness. At any rate they were there to fight.

In the morning Colonel Williamson, from his camp

THE WHITE SAVAGE

a mile from Gnadenhutten, ordered two squads to go ahead and reconnoiter. These sixteen men moved forward quietly towards the village. When they had got near to it they made out the figures of Indians in the cornfields over on the farther side of the Tuscarawas. Supposing that only a few would be there working they got hold of a hollowed-out log which had been used for catching maple sap and which made an excellent canoe. Two at a time they crossed to the other side.

But after getting farther into the cornfield they discovered that the Indians outnumbered them considerably. So without any show of hostility they went up to them and told them that they had come to guide them to a more agreeable place, a place where the Christian Delawares would thenceforth be kept in provisions and protected from all enemies—perhaps Fort Pitt. And as few Delawares, either Christian or Great Spiritist in their religious beliefs, would have objected to an arrangement which insured them food without working and security without fighting, it is not bewildering that the Indian men gave up their guns and tomahawks and followed their guides calmly. The women and children, shouldering the bundles of corn, prepared to follow.

In Gnadenhutten had been left that morning only one man and one squaw. These the main body under Colonel Williamson came upon when they entered the

THOSE DAMNED MISSIONARIES

town, which was a short time after the two advance squads had crossed the river. The man and the squaw were promptly shot. Their bodies lay in the village road while Colonel David Williamson sat down to await the return of the reconnoitering party who had crossed the creek and gone into the cornfields.

They came a little later, herding the meek Christian Delawares before them. Their arms were filled with the guns and tomahawks of these people even as the arms of the Indians were filled with ears of corn. Williamson met them pleasantly and after a time they agreed to be guided by the American officer's advice. They would, he told them, be taken somewhere and cared for. After this an Indian runner was sent down to Salem to inform the other Delawares of the arrangement and to bring them up to Gnadenhutten.

When the runner had disappeared Colonel Williamson's hundred men became more active. They walked lithely among the Indian men and women and began separating them like cattle. They bound their hands securely. Then the men were driven into one cabin and the women and children into another. It was too late for the Indians to cry out or to attempt an escape.

When the Christianized Delawares from Salem arrived they also were disarmed and thrust into the cabins. The number of prisoners so neatly taken stood at ninety-six, half a dozen of them being Wyandots who had accompanied the cornhusking party.

With the Indians from the two villages secured inside the cabins behind barred doors Colonel Williamson stood outside on the frozen trail and asked the rank and file that surrounded him, "Boys, which shall we do, kill them or take them back to Fort Pitt?"

Eighty-two of the hundred frontiersmen were of the opinion that the best thing to do was to kill them. Doubtless some of them offered the remark that the only good Indian was a dead Indian. . . . The sentence thus passed on them was soon made known to the victims.

It has been written often that among these Delawares whom the Moravians had been instructing in religion for many years were those who had made raids across the Ohio to the border; that militiamen saw bloodsplotched clothing which they wore and recognized the pieces as belonging to murdered friends of theirs; that some of the ninety-six doomed prisoners had been trailed from the scene of one of their depredations (which would seem impossible, considering the time of year and the distance involved); and all of those explanations of what followed may be true. But what cannot be explained away is the fact that Williamson's men were as murderous, as sickeningly lustful as any savage tribe ever known to the Ohio country.

THOSE DAMNED MISSIONARIES

On the morning of the next day, with scalping knives, mallets, tomahawks and spears, Williamson's hundred men divided between the doors of the cabins and went inside among the men, women and children. There they began a butchery that lasted—well, whatever length of time is required for the crude dismemberment of ninety-six human beings by means of ordinary weapons.

As for sidelights on the massacre there is one from Doddridge's Notes: "One woman, who could speak good English, knelt before the commander and begged his protection." (It seems that Williamson chose to deliver his blows among the women.) "Her supplication was unavailing." All then prepared for death and "the orisons of these devoted people were already ascending the throne of the Most High!—the sound of the Christian's prayer found an echo in the surrounding wood, but no responsive feeling in the bosoms of their executioners." And George Loskiel, presiding Bishop of the American Moravian Church from 1802 till 1811, supplies the following from the Tuscarawas County history: "Abraham, whose long, flowing hair had the day before attracted notice and elicited the remark that it would 'make a fine scalp,' was the first victim. One of the party, seizing a cooper's mallet, exclaimed, 'How exactly this will answer the business!' Beginning with

THE WHITE SAVAGE

Abraham he felled fourteen to the ground, then handed the instrument to another, saying, 'My arm fails me; go on in the same way. I think I have done pretty well.' "

While this wholesale execution was going on, the missionaries who had instructed these luckless Delawares in the ways of Christ were at Lower Sandusky, waiting for a boat to take them across Lake Erie to Detroit. For a letter in answer to the Half King's had come from Major De Peyster, who had given orders for them to be brought safely to the British western stronghold.

Wherein Vengeance Carelessly Takes the Wrong Man

CHAPTER VII

Wherein Vengeance Carelessly Takes the Wrong Man

THERE was a sequel to the massacre of the Indians in the Moravian missions. During the time it was in preparation Simon Girty roamed widely through the Ohio country, scouting, raiding and making discoveries with regard to proposed movements of American troops on the frontier. Though haunted by the fear of being taken by Pennsylvania or Virginia militiamen, nevertheless he had the hardihood to strike into their country at the head of Indian warriors.

Williamson's annihilation of the Christianized Delawares disturbed Girty, not because the deed had been so vilely cruel, but because it was a threat against his own safety. And he might have reflected that if it had not been for the white missionaries the Delaware territory would not now be so ragged as a defensive barrier against the Americans. He might have told himself that had it not been for Heckewelder, Zeisberger and the other Moravian brothers the Delawares would have stood a better chance of remaining a united tribe throughout the war, that these men had turned Chief White Eyes against his own people and by thus making a division among the Delawares had weakened the power of all the warriors. This had enabled the Pennsylvanians to move safely into the Indian country and to build Fort Laurens and Fort McIntosh, which they would otherwise have found it difficult to do. That had been partly the work of long-faced Heckewelder. And certainly the authorities at Pittsburgh had been kept well informed of intended Indian and British movements against them. This, too, had come from Heckewelder and the others. He might have said, Damn Heckewelder and Zeisberger and the whole lot of them! In fact, he did say it.

A few days after Colonel Williamson had burned the cabins above the piles of dead bodies at Gnadenhutten, Girty went up from the Half King's town to Lower Sandusky. There he discovered the missionaries. They were still waiting for the boat which Major De Peyster had sent them from Detroit and in which they were to be taken from the Indian country. As if, thought Girty, when he heard of this means of transportation that had been prepared for them,—as if these damned rascals were too good to walk! But then De Peyster and Hamilton before him had queer notions of treating people. They knew they were in a war, knew also (at least they had been told so often enough) that the missionaries were working directly for American interests, yet they

VENGEANCE TAKES THE WRONG MAN

would permit no harm to be done to these men. It was hard for Girty to understand how these Moravian brothers deserved this consideration.

He reached Lower Sandusky one night and sat down to a bottle of rum with a friend. The missionaries were housed in a nearby cabin. At every drink his irritation against them grew. If only he had his way about it they would carry a few marks on them by which to remember the Indian country when they left! And finally, when the rum was half gone, he took the bottle by the neck and lurched out into the chill spring night towards the cabin in which the missionaries were lying.

Heckewelder was trying to sleep, but couldn't. His face frowned nervously up into the darkness, for he was anxious to leave and fearful that the boat should not come before Girty arrived. Always there was this worry of his that Girty was about to kill him.

After a while Heckewelder heard Girty's voice boom out. He was talking to Le Villier, a flannel-mouthed French trader with whom he had never been on good terms, who had been given the task of guiding the missionaries to Lower Sandusky. Le Villier now sat by a candle in a room adjacent to that in which the missionaries were lying. They began to wrangle over Heckewelder and Zeisberger, and Girty cursed Le Villier and struck out at him.

THE WHITE SAVAGE

But soon Girty's attention was turned towards the men in the next room. It was they that he then cursed. The damned rascals! he said; and added drunkenly that he would never leave the cabin until he had split all of their heads with his tomahawk. And Heckewelder, though shivering with fear, yet felt his religious sense outraged by the luxuriousness of Girty's curses.

Girty swore and reeled and drank till after midnight. "I omit the names he called us by," wrote Heckewelder, "and the words he made use of while swearing, as also the place he would go to [it must have been Hell!] if he did not fulfill all which he had sworn that he would do to us. He had somewhere procured liquor, and would, as we were told by those who were near him, at every drink renew his oaths, which he repeated till he fell asleep.

"Never before did any of us hear the like oaths, or know anybody to rave like him. He appeared like an host of evil spirits. He would sometimes come up to the bolted door between us and him, threatening to chop it in pieces to get at us. No Indian we had ever seen drunk would have been a match for him. How we should escape the clutches of this white beast in human form no one could foresee . . ."

Yet the miracle was performed and Heckewelder and his associates were saved. In the morning at day-

VENGEANCE TAKES THE WRONG MAN

break two large, clumsy scows appeared from the west along the shores of Lake Erie and came to rest in the forest surrounded harbor of Lower Sandusky. That was joyful news for the missionaries. According to Heckewelder, they were at last satisfied that they would be "relieved from the hands of this wicked white savage, whose equal, we were led to believe, was not to be found among mankind."

As the boats turned about towards Detroit again Girty was doubtless sleeping off his drunkenness of the night before.

A short while later Girty left Lower Sandusky for the town of Captain Pipe on the Tymochtee. For there was more talk of an expedition of Pennsylvania militiamen against the Indians of northeastern Ohio and there was much to discuss with regard to it. Girty wanted direct news from the border and, assisted by a party of Delaware and Wyandot braves, he intended to go after it.

On his way to Captain Pipe's town he saw a white youth sitting disconsolately on a fallen log that lay in the forest. It was young Christian Fast who had been taken by Captain Brant and George Girty when they ambushed Colonel Lochry and destroyed most of his soldiers. Fast was seventeen and for some months he had been living as an adopted son of a Delaware family.

THE WHITE SAVAGE

But the ways of the Indian were strange to him; he could speak only a few words of their language and his longing again to be home among his own people was almost overpowering. Girty noticed him and asked as he drew nearer, "Boy, what are you thinking about?"

Young Fast looked up startled, then answered confusedly that he was lonesome because he had no company.

Girty gazed thoughtfully at him for a while. Finally he shook his head and observed sympathetically that what young Fast was longing for was not company but his people at home. "You be a good boy," he advised him, "and you'll get back there some day."

He went on to the village of Captain Pipe. Here he was joined by Scotosh, a son of the Half King and by eighty other Indians with whom he purposed going on a war party against the settlements. It was to be less of an attack than a scouting expedition; and Girty carried a message from Major De Peyster which he was to deliver to a British sympathizer within the American frontier.

They set out on the seventeenth of March for the Pennsylvania border. But when they had crossed the Ohio River Girty discovered that there were so many white men moving in groups through the woods that he would be unable to go much farther without attracting

VENGEANCE TAKES THE WRONG MAN

their attention. Therefore he had to turn away from his objective, the message undelivered, and seek out a new one.

To make a quick attack somewhere and push off hurriedly was what he decided to do. And after some days more his party found an accessible stockade. Creeping up towards it, they killed one of the soldiers and took another man prisoner. It was in the neighborhood of Fort Pitt, and the captured white man told Girty that General Irvine had been absent from Fort Pitt, attending a meeting of Congress, but that he was back again and on his return had called a war council of all the regular and militia officers. The purpose of the council was to discuss the advisability of a campaign against the Indians in northeastern Ohio and the result was that five hundred or more mounted Pennsylvanians were to gather at Fort McIntosh and from there push off on an attack upon the Wyandots and Delawares about Sandusky.

But Girty was not alarmed by this information which the prisoner had given him and which he sent on to Major De Peyster. The Indians were working closely with him and the Ohio country was astir. War parties which he had supplied with ammunition had gone out against the border and had returned with numerous scalps, but with only four of their own men as casual-

THE WHITE SAVAGE

ties. Moreover, none of the scalps on this occasion belonged to women or children, which rather pleased him.

With plans to meet the attacking force of Americans when they came, he moved northward to Upper Sandusky, taking with him "one hundred pounds of powder and two hundred pounds of ball, and eight dozen of knives for the use of the Wyandots, Monseys and Delawares. I [Girty] was obliged to purchase some little necessaries from Mr. Arundell [Arundle; he was a British trader among the Wyandots] that were not in the King's store, which I hope you will be good enough to excuse, as I did it for the good of the service. I should be very much obliged if you would be good enough to order me out some few stores, that I may have it in my power to give a little to some Indians that I know to be deserving . . ."

Girty, then, was at this time working soberly for the men on whose side he had chosen to fight. That he was capable of hatred and of sustaining it is probable, but the picture of him as a mad man who dashed out of the wilderness with a pack of howling braves, swooped down upon unprotected settlers and either tomahawked them on the spot or carried them back to some Indian village where he gleefully watched their bodies crisp and shrivel under the fire of the stake—the picture generally encountered of Girty and wholly accepted by

VENGEANCE TAKES THE WRONG MAN

most western writers (whole hog by Theodore Roosevelt and to an enormous extent by even so thoughtful a man as Butterfield) has only the vaguest outlines. It is true that he fought the borderers and went against armies sent out from the border, but there is no proof to show that when the issue was decided he set exultantly to work on the skulls of the prisoners or abetted the Indians in their torturous executions.

Already, however, he had done enough to be remembered by many a borderer who had never even seen him. But, though he had deserted the Americans, though he had led many a maraud into Pennsylvania and Virginia and Kentucky, and though Heckewelder left a record of his unique and cruel character, he might have been forgotten by the popular mind had it not been for one event. That event had been shaping up since the day of the Moravian massacre and was an indirect outcome of it. It took place in the early summer of 1782.

As early as April of that year news had seeped into the Ohio country that an expedition was being planned at Fort Pitt against the Wyandots. Girty had discovered it from the prisoner he had taken some time before. Parties of Indians out hunting or scouting saw it verified in the extraordinary movements of the white men along the east bank of the Ohio.

The attack on Coshocton and the breakup of Salem,

THE WHITE SAVAGE

Gnadenhutten and Schönbrunn had caused the Delawares to take up new abodes farther from the frontier; the killing of the Christian Indians had sent them yet farther into the wilderness, so that now both Delawares and Wyandots intermingled between Upper and Lower Sandusky. At Captain Pipe's town on the Tymochtee there was a host of the former. And among them were cousins, uncles and other relations of the Christianized Indians who had been massacred. At the camp of the war chief Wingenund there were more. Thus the Indians about the Sandusky plains, where the coarse grassy land was spotted with islets of soft wood, were made morose and vindictive not only by the threatened invasion of their land and destruction of their fields and cabins but also by the remembrance of the past, principally the picture of ninety Delawares hacked and burned in Gnadenhutten. Considerable spirit was waiting to be shown in that territory.

Girty was at the Half King's town on the Sandusky when word was brought that a force of men had left Fort Pitt and was gathering near the borderline made by the Ohio River. Knowing at once the destination of that army, the Sandusky Indians made preparations to meet them. Half King and Girty sent a runner to Detroit asking Major De Peyster for help. And while the British officer was getting ready the Faith to sail

VENGEANCE TAKES THE WRONG MAN

down the river and across Lake Erie with rangers under Captain William Caldwell, Girty and the chiefs sounded the alarm to distant Wyandots, Delawares, Shawanese and Mingoes.

As these preparations were being made to meet them the Pennsylvania volunteers crossed the Ohio and encamped at Mingo Bottom, near what is now Steubenville but which was once a Mingo village. They were well mounted and equipped, but had had no training in acting under one commander. Among them were most of the hundred men who had slaughtered the helpless Christian Delawares at Gnadenhutten a few months earlier. The commander of that party—Colonel David Williamson—was also present. And for a time it was thought that he would lead this new expedition as he had the old. For wasn't it under his leadership that the borderers had been enabled to kill ninety-six Indians? And wasn't that sufficient to make him stand out as a man of parts?

But fortunately for Williamson there was another officer of the same rank present. He was Colonel William Crawford, a more decent, more likable, and more respectable soldier than the man who had distinguished himself at Gnadenhutten. The choice of commander was made by popular election and Crawford received the most votes from the five hundred mounted volunteers.

THE WHITE SAVAGE

He was the man to lead them to destroy the Wyandot towns.

From the day the Pennsylvania militiamen arrived at Mingo Bottom they were watched by the people whom they meant to attack. But in ignorance of this they rode forward, striking the same trail which Williamson had followed three months earlier, and continuing to the Tuscarawas where they saw the burned cabins and the trampled fields of Gnadenhutten, the cabins which some of the men in the party remembered firing into crematories for the bodies of Indians which they had dismembered.

Here they were seen again by Wyandot or Delaware spies. But this time the discovery was mutual. Three of Colonel Crawford's men on a foraging party some distance from the main camp (where their horses were being fed on Indian corn) discerned the figures of two braves. The militiamen immediately fired. But their marksmanship was poor and the two braves fled unharmed. However, at the sound of the shot nearly half the volunteers—two hundred and fifty, that would be—came tumbling out of camp with their flintlocks loaded, ready to be on hand for what they took to be the beginning of a lively skirmish.

But nothing happened. The two braves vanished and the forest was still again save for the noises of the

VENGEANCE TAKES THE WRONG MAN

four hundred and eighty Pennsylvanians as they made fires and cooked their provisions along the banks of the Tuscarawas. Night came, then another day, and they rode farther into the wilderness towards Sandusky.

Several days passed. It was the fifth of June, 1782. Crawford's force followed its guides out upon a branch of the Sandusky by whose banks there had once been a Moravian village. The cabins were there, but deserted. There were dark rings on the lush green ground where fires had been. But it was all so quiet, so ominously quiet. The volunteers might have heard the undisturbed echoes of their own voices.

In the tall grass about the empty village they could find only their own tracks. Questions came up to be settled by the officers and the wiseacres of the Indian country: Which way had the damned redskins gone? How much farther could they go before striking the Wyandot braves? How strong would the Indian force be when they finally did make contact with it? And hadn't they better retreat? Finally it was decided that the Pennsylvanians would march one day longer towards the west and then, if no Delawares or Wyandots were encountered, they would turn back from this silent prairie land.

Three days earlier Captain William Caldwell with his Canadian rangers and a number of northern Indians had arrived at the Half King's town on the Sandusky to join Girty and a band of Wyandots, Captain Pipe and Wingenund with the Delawares, and a band of Mingoes besides. Gathering the whole force under him— even then it was considerably smaller than Crawford's— Caldwell set out to challenge the advance of the Pennsylvania militiamen.

They met on the afternoon of June 6 in a land of tall grass studded with clumps of trees. The fighting began when an advance party of braves, creeping low over the ground, came suddenly within sight of Crawford's scouts and instantly discharged their muskets. The scouts retired, but were jostled forward by Crawford's main body. Meanwhile Captain Caldwell and several sections of men under him were entering a large grove that dominated the plain. It became a contested spot as Colonel Crawford's volunteers rode up. And in the rip and whine of musketry that announced the general engagement Caldwell was struck by a leaden ball and had to be carried away from the ensuing action. The Pennsylvanians lost one captain, who was killed, and two captains and a major, who were wounded.

The Americans gained the grove and drove the British and Indians out of it, into the tall grass. Then both sides formed lines and faced each other at a complete standstill.

VENGEANCE TAKES THE WRONG MAN

It was a curious situation. The Canadians and Indians knew the American number to be much greater than theirs and so hesitated to take the offensive, especially as they were expecting reinforcements from the Shawanese. But the Pennsylvanians had been unable to find out the size of the enemy. Discovering white troops among them—which they had not counted on—they believed that the Canadians and Indians mustered at least double their own number. So throughout the long afternoon both sides kept a respectful distance from each other and passed the time by a not too expert show of marksmanship.

Night came. In the darkness bonfires were laid and lighted in front of the waiting men, lighted so that the glow from the burning wood might save either from a surprise attack. The antagonists lay on their arms and fought with gnats and mosquitoes which buzzed and bit viciously and continuously. The sunrise the next morning disclosed Americans, Canadians and Indians to be lying exactly where they had been the night before.

If Colonel Crawford, instead of wasting this period of darkness, had made an early attack and had been able to keep his men under control the story would have had a different ending. He would have been glad to, asserts Butterfield, but, as that authority explains, there were "several obstacles in the way; several of his men were sick and a number had been wounded"—which is so poor an excuse that it makes one want to search for a good one, an explanation better than the obvious fact that Crawford let the momentous dawn slip by because his command of his troops was not strong enough to send them forward.

As the day brightened all hope was lost. For Pennsylvanian and Indian watchers observed coming over the rippling grass to the south and west a band of mounted warriors—one hundred and forty Shawanese whom Alexander McKee had brought hurriedly up from Wapatomica. And now, with both forces about equal even with these additional men on the Indian side, Crawford's officers came together for a "war council," the upshot of which was that they would hold their lines until nightfall and then make a quick but orderly retreat through the darkness.

Here it might be expected that, strengthened by so many Shawanese warriors, the Canadians and Indians would take the battle in their own hands. Instead they too remained on the defensive, sending over only enough shot to keep in mind that an enemy lay before them. The day went slowly and unprofitably by.

In the darkness the order for the retreat was passed. All along the American line men stood up, took their equipment and hurried towards the trail that wound to

VENGEANCE TAKES THE WRONG MAN

the south and west. They did not attempt to form into any kind of marching order; they simply streamed in the general direction of where they wanted to go—where safety lay.

But Crawford, as he should have done, stood by. He wanted to see that nobody was left. And as the men passed him he called out the names of four about whom he was particularly anxious: John Crawford, his son; Major Harrison, his son-in-law; and his nephews, Major Rose and young William Crawford. But they did not answer him. He waited, growing nervous.

In the confusion Crawford was left behind. For with all speed the gallant Williamson had put himself at the head of about three hundred men and led them to the trail. Crawford wandered about in the darkness, calling now and then in a low voice. After a while he was answered by Dr. Knight, the regimental surgeon. More voices of stragglers sounded and a small group thus came together.

They struck directly eastward, missing the trail. There was not a guide—quite naturally—in the party of men left behind. Blindly and fatally they plodded towards the village of Wingenund, the Delaware war-chief, but thinking they were moving towards the south and east where safety lay. For two long days these men

THE WHITE SAVAGE

wandered about through tall grass, cranberry marshes and woodland.

Williamson, however, had better luck. Beginning the retreat he led three hundred of the militiamen to the Sandusky River and followed down the east bank. It was not till morning that he discovered that Colonel Crawford, the regimental surgeon, Crawford's son-in-law, Major Harrison, and his nephew, William Crawford, as well as a number of enlisted men, were missing. But despite this he led on the retreat; was hastened some time during the day when a few mounted rangers and Indians overtook them and drove them from the rear. Williamson halted long enough to meet them. He lost three men killed and eight wounded, but repelled the attack successfully. Five days later he was on the home side of the Ohio River.

But by this time Crawford, Dr. Knight, a man named Slover, and some others were in the hands of the Delawares. Muddy from wading the cranberry marshes, scratched and torn by the briars and half-starved, they had come out upon a trail on the afternoon of June 7 and there had met a party of Delawares who were returning from their pursuit of Williamson. The American commander was badly worn by his two days and nights of wandering. He made little resistance. The Delawares closed about them with musket barrels bris-

VENGEANCE TAKES THE WRONG MAN

tling. Thongs were brought out and the Americans' hands were tied behind their backs. Then they were marched to the camp of Wingenund, from where, after three days' captivity, they were led under a heavy guard to Upper Sandusky.

From the moment he was taken by the Delawares Crawford's death was virtually certain. And the wonder is not that he died, but that he lived so long. Following closely after the well-remembered massacre by Williamson, carrying many of the men in his own army who had taken part in it, and being at the head of an invading force which had come to destroy the homes of the Wyandots and Delawares, he could have had little reasonable hope that mercy would be shown him.

Yet Crawford did have that hope. And hearing that Simon Girty, whom he had known and had doubtless considered an inferior while about Fort Pitt, was with the Half King at Upper Sandusky, he asked that his captors take him to the cabin of that Wyandot chief.

They agreed. Colonel Crawford and Simon Girty met in the Half King's town on the night of the tenth of June. Crawford was pale, badly scratched and weary. But though his own life was in the greatest of danger, his thoughts when he saw Girty were of his son-in-law, William Harrison, and of his brother's son who had been named for him. Both of these young men had lain with

THE WHITE SAVAGE

him near a clump of trees while facing the enemy on June 5, had been with him at the beginning of the retreat, but they also had got lost from the main body.

When Girty appeared Crawford's first question was of these two young men. They too had been taken by the Delawares, who had burned them at the stake at a village farther down the river. But this Girty did not tell to Crawford. Instead, either because he did not really know what had happened to them or because he felt it difficult to speak the true words, he said that they had been captured by the Shawanese, but that these warriors had pardoned them. Then Crawford and Girty talked a little longer, nobody knows about what; but it has been declared that Simon gave his word to intercede for the unfortunate colonel.

From here all evidence as to what Girty did or left undone is very shaky and contradictory. It is said that he tried to save Crawford; it is likewise said that he did nothing to save him. But both sides in discussing whether Girty did or did not attempt to free Crawford have slighted one important point.

It is generally taken for granted that Girty should have tried to save Crawford and that he was a fiend for not doing so. But why should he have done so? Because they were both white men? (In war white men had killed each other for centuries.) Because they had

VENGEANCE TAKES THE WRONG MAN

both lived at Fort Pitt? (In every important city to the east there were loyalists and patriots who later fought against each other.) Because common humanity demanded that Girty exert himself to prevent a burning party? (Then Common Humanity asked too much of the people of that time and place and should have known better.) In bolstering up reasons for what Girty should have done but omitted to do, western writers claim that the two men had been friends at Fort Pitt and that Girty had been frequently a guest "at Crawford's hospitable cabin" in Pennsylvania—a likely story, considering that one was then a major and a man of property while the other was a border roughneck with a taste for Indian life and the possessor of not a single foot of property in the world!

And if they were not friends why should Girty have tried to save him? And how could he have accomplished it even if he had tried?

Early in the morning after Crawford had been brought to Sandusky, Captain Pipe and Wingenund came to claim the prisoner. He belonged to them, had been taken by the Delawares whom he had tried to destroy. His fate, as Colonel John Johnston has summed it up, was "in satisfaction for the massacre of their people at the Moravian towns on the Muskingum." Captain Pipe met him and spoke to him from cruel lips;

he was glad to see Crawford, he said, and meanwhile stood over him with his hands full of a black, sticky mixture which he began to daub on Crawford's face—the death warrant.

From the Half King's town Captain Pipe and Wingenung took Crawford a few miles westward along the "old trace leading to the Big Spring, Wyandot town. It was on the right hand of the trace going west, on a low bottom on the east bank of the Tymochtee creek."

A fair-sized party wound up that trace with Crawford. Towards the head of it was the chief prisoner, bound and heavily guarded. Nearby rode Captain Pipe and Wingenund. A stone's throw back of these came Dr. Knight, the regimental surgeon, his hands tied and a Delaware brave on either side of him. Now and again there appeared from the opposite direction infuriated squaws, braves and boys, some of whom slapped wet scalps first in the blackened face of Crawford, then against the cheeks of little Dr. Knight. Stones flew out and struck the prisoners; furious braves lay cudgels on their backs. Screams and insults engulfed the party in a hideous sea of noise.

Among those riding eastward along the trace was Simon Girty. He had returned to the Delawares after his meeting with Crawford at the Half King's town. As he came slowly towards the party he stopped and

VENGEANCE TAKES THE WRONG MAN

talked to Crawford, then rode on. Coming up to Dr. Knight he asked, "Is this the doctor?"

"Yes," Knight answered, and held out his hand in belated friendship.

"You're a damned rascal; get the hell along there," Girty told him in effect, but later added (and this was not an unkindness) that Knight was to be taken to the Shawanese towns.

The stake was already standing; a small blaze was creeping slowly along the faggots that encircled it, and about a hundred Delawares, with a few from other tribes, sat watching expectantly when the prisoners arrived.

"When we were come to the fire," Knight wrote afterward, having been transferred to another town and making his escape on the way, "the colonel was stripped naked, ordered to sit down by the fire, and then they beat him with sticks and their fists. Presently after, I was treated in the same manner. They then tied a rope to the foot of a post about fifteen feet high, bound the colonel's hands behind his back and fastened the rope to the ligature between his wrists. The rope was long enough for him to sit down or walk around the post once or twice and return the same way. The Colonel then called to Girty and asked if they intended to burn him. Girty answered, yes. The colonel said he would take it all patiently. Upon this Captain Pipe made a speech to the Indians, viz., about thirty or forty men, sixty or seventy squaws or boys. When the speech was ended they all yelled a hideous and hearty assent to what had been said."

What Captain Pipe said is easily imagined. He spoke of the treachery of Brodhead's campaign when the Delawares were driven from Coshocton, of the Moravian massacre and of his latest attempt by the prisoner at the stake to send the Delawares fleeing still farther into the wilderness. Now Pipe and Wingenund had their revenge.

Meanwhile Girty stood watching. Perhaps by that time he had become so dulled to executions of this kind that he could look on Crawford without once imagining himself to be standing in his place; perhaps he had taken from the Indians their own feelings with regard to scenes of torture—that it is the test of a brave man and to be watched with scorn or admiration, depending on whether the victim cries out or is proud in his fortitude. But that he had come there to take conscious pleasure in the slow death of Crawford is too much to assert without more proof than there is at hand. It is quite as likely that no ill will towards Crawford brought him there and that once among the hot-blooded braves and squaws he wished he could find himself suddenly taken

VENGEANCE TAKES THE WRONG MAN

elsewhere. For circumstances made him cut an embarrassing figure that he could not have escaped noticing and forced him into a position from which writers on early frontier history have inferred that he was a monster.

While the surrounding braves were shooting powder into Crawford's naked skin, while burning faggots were thrust against his sides and the scalping knife shaved his ears off clean he came close to the end of his endurance and called out to Girty, whom he begged to shoot him. But Girty did not answer; there was no sensible answer he could make. If he had complied there would have been a hundred braves and squaws, maddened at being cheated of their vengeance, upon him; and evidently he could not bring himself flatly to deny Crawford his request.

Crawford called again. And this time Girty turned away and with a laugh, as Dr. Knight reported (though there are many kinds of laughter and not all of them are delighted, humorous or gay), "he said that he had no gun . . ."

People who read of this ghastly performance—people excepting Indians, of course—naturally sympathize with Colonel Crawford. A competent enough and decent enough man himself, he had come on the heels of Williamson's murderous expedition, had brought a gang

THE WHITE SAVAGE

of border rough necks whom he could not control, had been left behind by his own outfit and had given himself into the hands of the very tribes whose means of subsistence he had come to destroy and whose braves he meant to kill. His burning is a scene which warms the blood of every patriotic American, yes, and blinds the eye. For he had no right to expect to live; and if the Delawares had spared him they would have shown themselves so much more humane than the average borderer of that day that the contrast would even now be painful. As it was, though the Pennsylvanians, Virginians and Kentuckians fought as brutally and killed as indiscriminately as the Indian, they appear to have been more civilized than their darker brother in that they never brought torture up to a really fine art in their daily lives . . .

After a while Crawford's body lay still and black and the flames ran low over the expiring faggots.

With One War Ended and None Other at Hand Simon Takes a Wife

CHAPTER VIII

With One War Ended and None Other at Hand
Simon Takes a Wife

*T*HE next year ended the War of the Revolution. But when word finally reached the border that peace had been declared between Great Britain and the United States of America, Simon Girty, characteristically, was leading a marauding party to within a few miles of Pittsburgh. He heard the guns which the commandant at Fort Pitt was firing in salute to these tidings, but he could not believe that these dull, sullen booms that shook the quiet of the countryside were made in joyous recognition that the war had ended. A prisoner he had captured there plaintively told him that peace between the two countries had come, but Girty remained dubious and took him back to Detroit in spite of his remonstrances.

Earlier, in the fall of 1782 and the spring of 1783, Simon had fought steadily against the frontiersmen. With Captain Caldwell's Canadian rangers and Alexander McKee's Indians he had been at the battle of Blue Licks and had been in the attack on Bryan's Station.

THE WHITE SAVAGE

Besides engaging in these he had led some expeditions of his own against the Kentucky and Virginia borders. It seems he was ready to continue fighting indefinitely.

But when he reached Detroit from his last maraud during the war he discovered that there were no more attacks just then to be taken part in. The British commandant, instead of locking up the prisoner which Girty had brought from Fort Pitt, released him and returned him to his home. There was peace! Affairs had quieted down! It was difficult for him to understand, but after a while he mastered it.

It was during this unaccountable lull that Simon made a slight concession to civilization. He married Miss Catharine Malott, a girl of about half his age.

In an April four years earlier Catharine, her young brothers and sisters and her parents were on their way down the Ohio River towards the Kentucky settlements. They had passed a little beyond Wheeling when a band of Indians appeared and began firing. The father, Peter Malott, managed to escape. But the rest of the family was captured and began to live the life of the Indians.

When Simon met her, Catharine had become the adopted daughter in an offshoot family of the Delawares. She wore moccasins, a leather petticoat and she greased herself well with bear fat, a process warranted to protect her skin from the stings and bites of outrageous insects. When they met and why they married can only be conjectured. Perhaps it was a love affair. Or perhaps Catharine so abominated the Indian mode of life that, as her only chance of escape, she was willing to accept Simon Girty. At any rate, in August, 1784, she left the Indian village in which she had grown to young womanhood and followed her intended husband up through the Ohio country and around the west shore of Lake Erie to Detroit.

At the beginning marriage made a change in Simon's wandering life. He talked with some of the Indians across the river from Detroit—for he needed a respectable place to live—and asked them whether they minded if he laid out a little farm along the east bank of the river. They were willing for him to come. But he also got permission from the British commandant, who was very strict with white men who trespassed on Indian country. So Simon built a cabin a few rods south of where the Canadian village of Malden grew up, and began thinking of cultivating the soil into a farm. Retired on half pay from the British Indian service, he and Catharine lived in their stout cabin with no pressing wants unsatisfied.

But of this kind of existence he was to know very little.

THE WHITE SAVAGE

The peace that had come seriously affected only the east. On the western border, from Fort Pitt down to the Kentucky country and along the broadening Ohio, affairs continued virtually as they had been before. In one article of the treaty between England and America the former was given the right to all of the trading posts of the Great Lakes region as security until America had paid off her obligations to loyalists whose goods the government had taken. This enabled the British Indian service to keep its hold on the Ohio tribes, which was necessary if Canadian traders were to continue their profitable business in the exchange of furs. It was to their interest that the Ohio tribes remain where they were. And this, quite naturally, was also what the Indian himself wanted. But in opposition to both of them the Americans were already beginning to look on the rich land northwest of the Ohio as belonging to themselves and to make efforts towards securing it.

The same year in which Simon Girty married Catharine Malott and went to live near Malden there was held the treaty of Fort Stanwix between the Americans and the Seneca-Iroquois confederacy. But to give theå name of treaty to what took place is to misuse the word. For the United States commissioners simply demanded what they wanted and the Indians were forced to accept. The situation is thus explained in the History of the

SIMON TAKES A WIFE

Territory Northwest of the Ohio: "Large bounties of land had been promised by Congress to officers and soldiers of the line (the same practice that had caused Lord Dunmore's War in 1774). Virginia, who regarded herself as owner of the unlimited territories of Tennessee and Kentucky and northwest of the Ohio, had also made magnificent promises of bounties to her soldiers and officers. These bounties in case of brigadier generals were 10,000 acres; and to major generals, 15,000 acres; all other officers less, in proportion to their rank. Those who were entitled to these bounties became anxious to receive them. By the war their business had been broken up, the commerce and manufactures of the country were of little value, and the small and sterile farms of New England and the Atlantic coast offered small attractions for agriculture compared with the rich lands of Kentucky and the Ohio country, of which accounts had found their way to these eastern states. Congress was pressed by them to provide for the settlement of these territories, particularly the great region northwest of the Ohio River. Believing that the Indian tribes who had been at war with the United States were to be treated as defeated enemies, with no absolute rights in the lands they occupied, Congress made the treaty of Fort Stanwix in October, 1784, with the Six Nations, fixing their boundary west by the west line of Pennsylvania and giving to the United States all north and west of the Ohio."

A few months later another arbitrary treaty was made, that of Fort McIntosh, in which the Delawares and Wyandots signed away not only land that did belong to them but land that was not theirs as well. And thus it was taken for granted that the Ohio country was freely open to colonization and that if the Indians did not peaceably submit they were treacherous scoundrels and deserved no pity.

But the Indians would not submit, at least not without a fight. And this brought Simon Girty down into the Ohio country again before his marriage had run a year. For the British Indian service, seeing the situation, also saw that they could make use of it to keep their valuable trading posts.

Simon, McKee, and Matthew Elliott became the three principal agents in the Ohio country who kept the Indian temper at war heat. In the spring of 1785 Colonel Josiah Harmar, then commandant at Fort McIntosh, learned of Girty's movements and sputtered, "Speeches have been continually sent by the British from Detroit to the Indians since the treaty, and I have good intelligence that several traders have been among them, using all means to make them entertain a bad opinion of the Americans. One Simon Girty, I am informed, has been to Sandusky for that purpose. I have taken every means in my power to counteract their proceedings, and have directed the Indians not to listen to their lies, but to tie and bring in here any of those villains who spread reports among them injurious to the United States, in order that they may be punished."

Colonel Harmar (later General Harmar, who was to lead a large and unsuccessful expedition against these Indians who had the effrontery to listen to bad opinions spoken of the United States) here breathes the very spirit of the men who stood impatiently waiting to break through the Indian border. Like George Rogers Clark at Vincennes, like the commissioners at Forts Stanwix and McIntosh he did not confer with the natives, he *directed* them. It was villainous that a bad opinion of the Americans should be spread among the Indians. The Indians should take all of the men who talked injuriously of the United States, tie them and hand them over to American justice! And meanwhile all of their land was being confiscated.

Girty, however, was not taken to Fort McIntosh to be punished. He continued to roam the Ohio country widely, going among the Delawares, Wyandots and Shawanese, giving them counsel and presents. And despite the directions of Colonel Harmar he was allowed to continue his damaging work among the tribes.

THE WHITE SAVAGE

The treaty of Fort Stanwix had penned up the Seneca-Iroquois; the treaty of Fort McIntosh had halved the land of the Delawares, and now the Shawanese and Miamis were in line to be treated with, for immigration was swinging down the Ohio. So a fort was built at the mouth of the Great Miami and in the fall of 1785 the Indians of southern and western Ohio were invited to hear how much land was to be left them; or, as Butterfield puts it, "Congress [was of the opinion] that the treaty of peace of 1783 with Great Britain absolutely invested the [American] government with the fee of all the Indian lands within the limits of the United States and that they had the right to assign or retain such portions as they should judge proper."

But the Indians thought otherwise. And the only representatives that came to Fort Finney were a few Shawanese. Nevertheless they were told that thenceforth their hunting grounds were to begin far north of the Ohio River, to go west into the country claimed by the Miamis and south and east to the boundaries of the Wyandots and Delawares.

The Shawanese chiefs went back to their families, looking angrily at the string of wampum which the Americans had given them. As for the Miamis, they had kept proudly aloof. Until now, because they were the farthest westward tribe in the Ohio country, they

SIMON TAKES A WIFE

had not been troubled by the headlong rushing settlers. But their turn was soon to come.

Despite these treaties, the strings of wampum and the presentation of hostages which accompanied them, the Indians were not satisfied to lose their land. On the Tuscarawas and the Hockhocking in the northeast white men fell under the tomahawk; and at the new headquarters of the Delawares near Wapatomica there was held a great council of Wyandots, Shawanese, Delawares, Miamis and others who came to discuss ways of driving out the Americans. They had been temporarily stunned into inactivity when England had given up the war. But now they were rallying again, even though the colonies had faced about from east to west.

England, they found, was still willing to help them and Sir John Johnson, they were told, was to hold a council for their benefit in the following year—it was 1786—at Niagara. It would be chiefly among the Seneca-Iroquois, but the Ohio Indians were invited to be present. Ready for any alliance they could find, they came; and at the meeting Girty, McKee, and Elliott helped strengthen their resolve to make whoever took their lands pay for them in some way or other.

At this council Johnson truthfully told the assembled sachems and warriors that if the various tribes did not unite in a solid front of defense they would soon lose all of their hunting grounds. Many heard him, many cheered, but nothing was done about it.

Another meeting was held by Johnson later in the year. The place was up the Detroit River from Lake Erie and representatives of more than a dozen tribes came there. Captain Brant arrived from the east and heatedly harangued the assembly on the necessity of an all-embracing confederacy to repel the whites. But through a variety of interests and dialects which gave them much to overcome they were enabled to act together only slightly: as a body they notified Congress that they expected settlers to keep out of the Ohio country and asked that the United States send commissioners to meet them near the Ohio boundary to discuss the future relations between the two races. The coming spring (1787), they thought, would be a good time for the council to take place.

The coming spring, the Americans thought, was a better time to think of settling the Ohio country with white men. A portion of the southern part had been surveyed and in that year Congress placed enough on sale in New York to amount to $72,974. And in the fall of the year Manasseh Cutler and Winthrop Sargeant, acting as agents for the New England Ohio Company, bought a tract that was bounded "by the Ohio, from the mouth of the Scioto to the intersection of the

Sir John Johnson

SIMON TAKES A WIFE

western boundary of the seventh range of townships then surveying; thence by said boundary to the northern boundary to the northern boundary or the tenth township from the Ohio; thence by a due west line to the Scioto; thence by the Scioto to the beginning." And in the same month that this land was sold Congress appointed a governor to the Northwest Territory. General Arthur St. Clair was chosen. There were a secretary and some judges, also an ordinance for the government of the territory, which last contains the curious statement that "the utmost good faith shall always be observed towards the Indians, their lands and property shall never be taken from them without their consent . . ."; as though anyone ever willingly consented to having his property taken from him. . . . A month later General Rufus Putnam, under the direction of the land company, had got forty-seven men and was making ready to go to this immense tract and prepare it for the settlers who were to follow.

That was the only answer the tribes received to their request that the Americans keep out of the Ohio country until after another council had been held. During the summer of 1787 the Indians, however, were expecting some news of the commissioners and had come to the foot of the Maumee Rapids to await it. Time went by and no message came; guided by Brant the representatives of the various tribes concluded they would return to their families and meet again in the following year at the same place.

Before this second convention of Indians there was another settlement of white men on the northwest side of the Ohio. John Cleve Symmes, father-in-law of William Henry Harrison, and a number of other land speculators had bought a tract between the Great and Little Miamis and within a month afterward had begun a settlement five miles above the site on which Cincinnati now stands.

Time came for the convention. But as the day approached a runner appeared at the foot of the Maumee Rapids with a message from Governor St. Clair. He had discovered that they were to meet again and in order to confuse them and divert them from any direct action they might take he requested that they meet him at Fort Harmar. Which was no more than a trick, for no sooner had the tribal sachems got halfway across the wilderness than they were met by another messenger from St. Clair who informed them that they would be foolish to expect the white man to recross the Ohio and that the early treaties must be abided by. Disgusted and angered, Brant and the rest turned back.

It was such events as these, all of them increasing the sullenness of the Indians—who saw themselves

SIMON TAKES A WIFE

hemmed in now to the east and south—and inflaming the warriors to a heat in which they flung themselves across the encroaching border and hacked at settlers, burning their cabins and stockades, which led up to the Indian war and which, in turn, enabled Simon Girty to pass what remained of his prime years in scenes of gore.

Wherein Two Generals Lose Their Armies

CHAPTER IX

Wherein Two Generals Lose Their Armies

By 1790 Catharine Girty had borne her husband two children, Ann and Thomas. And now Simon had all the things that makes a domesticated man. But though on the verge of fifty, having led an extraordinarily hard life, he was yet eager to leave his wife, his son and daughter, his farm and warm cabin and go off into the wilderness where he would sleep on a bed of skins, eat with his fingers in the Indian way and where he knew that war was imminent. For word had come that General Harmar (he commanded Fort Washington, the recently built garrison on the north bank of the Ohio near Symmes' settlement) had plans to march northward with more than a thousand men. That information, rather than holding Girty back, was what drew him down to the Ohio country.

Simon made his headquarters at the foot of the Maumee Rapids, a few miles up the bay from Lake Erie. The rapids were a long stretch of rock-studded shallows beside which the sachems and warriors who attended the Ohio Indian council of 1787 waited for the answer from General St. Clair, the answer that never came. They were well towards the mouth of the Maumee, which river hems in the extreme northwestern corner of what later became Ohio state. And it was in this corner that the tribes were congregating. Blue Jacket, the stubborn and courageous Shawanese chieftain, had a village along the Auglaize one mile from its junction with the Maumee; young Tecumseh was close at hand; Captain Pipe had come westward with his Delaware warriors and was hovering in the neighborhood; Tarhe the Crane and some Wyandots had a village within a day's journey to the east; while down at the Maumee's source, at the meeting of the St. Mary's and St. Joseph's rivers, Little Turtle was at Kekionggay, the seat of the Miami tribe. And during the year Captain Joseph Brant was thereabouts with some of his Mohawks.

The foot of the Maumee Rapids was then a busy place. Supplies of powder, muskets, lead, mutton, peas, corn, rice, blue, red, scarlet and crimson bolts of cloth, bags of vermilion dye, were being sent down by flatboat from Detroit, and Simon was at hand to apportion the goods among the various tribes. Old braves strode about in blankets, staring gloomily or with lighted eyes. Young bucks laughed and tried their muscles in the games, the broad jump, the running race and an early, almost pre-

TWO GENERALS LOSE THEIR ARMIES

historic kind of football in which one side tried to carry a stuffed and rounded skin through the other. The squaws watched their men folk and went quietly about their work of providing wood and water, which were plentiful. There was talk of war and of a great council meeting at which it would be determined.

The early fall of the year went by and news came than General Harmar was on his way. What did he think he was going to do? the Indians wondered. Simon Girty walked about among them, sometimes in the Indian dress, breeches, moccasins, a long skin shirt, silver bracelets on his wrists and earrings pendant along his round, sun-tanned cheeks. The Americans, he loudly repeated the Indians' thoughts, had no right to be on the north bank of the Ohio! Let them go back to where they belonged! With most of the braves he could speak in their own tongue and his voice was beginning to be heard in their council meetings, at which he was the only white man permitted.

For twelve years now Simon had been living in their villages and camps, attending and often leading bands of warriors against the border, supplying many of their wants from the King's stores. They knew him to have a fair amount of honesty and never to have cheated them. Many times he had led parties of them on bold marauds, and usually they had come back with scalps, prisoners

THE WHITE SAVAGE

and goods looted from white stockades and cabins. He had qualities which they admired—strength without foolhardiness, perseverance in war and the willingness to slash out fiercely against the enemy. For a long time he had continued his duties in the British service and his counsel to the Indians had always been for them to fight. Yet there was something more than mere duty or friendships to sharpen his thoughts towards war with the Americans. There was something personal about it; and this axe which he had to grind had been curiously fashioned.

So far as the United States was concerned Girty was an outlaw. Years earlier he and Alexander McKee and Matthew Elliott had been charged with treason by a continental court and when they did not appear had been adjudged guilty. Thus a legal execution waited for him in Pennsylvania. And this fact, perhaps inconsiderable by itself, fitted neatly in with the general American attitude towards him as he had learned it. It must have seemed to him that half the country which he had so surreptitiously left was imbued with the most bitter and personal hatred towards him. This knowledge had first come through chance, when he had captured the letter in which Colonel John Gibson had written coolly that if Girty fell into his hands he would trepan him. Up to that time, though he had had ample opportunity, he had

TWO GENERALS LOSE THEIR ARMIES

not been especially violent against the borderers. On returning with the letter to Detroit, however, he was gloomy, as Heckewelder noticed. Then there were Heckewelder's and Zeisberger's reports to Fort Pitt, from which it appeared that one Simon Girty, late of the Pittsburgh garrison, was one of the most ubiquitous and most malignant forces that preyed on the frontier. These, spreading about the facts of Girty's raids and exaggerating them, must have been in the minds—in fact they were—of many of the borderers whom Girty captured or met in the Indian villages. There was also a reward on his head: it was for eight hundred dollars, nearly as much as President Washington thought the Cherokees should receive as annuities for having been driven out of North Carolina! All this was fermenting in his mind. Even at the burning of Colonel Crawford he had been apprehensive of what the Americans would do to him if he fell into their hands. He asked the opinion of Dr. Knight on this point, muttering that he heard something about vengeance having been sworn against him. Then he had tried to make little of the matter by adding that for his part he doubted it. Plainly he was worried.

Now the Americans were coming, pushing bunglingly but irresistibly up through the long shadows of defeat. And from his headquarters at the Maumee Rap-

THE WHITE SAVAGE

ids Simon listened to the news brought by the fleet runners. General Harmar, it was discovered, had left Fort Washington in October with thirteen hundred men. He was aiming in the direction of the Miami villages about Kekiong-gay.

But this time Girty had no chance to meet the Americans. For Little Turtle, glowering but prudent, had withdrawn all of his warriors and their families. They had taken their belongings and had moved down the Maumee so as to be near the other tribes in case Harmar drove farther into their country. He would soon go back.

Harmar arrived. He found Kekiong-gay bare and deserted. About the empty cabins the cornstalks had been stripped. But he destroyed what little there was to be destroyed and then turned back towards Fort Washington.

But his return march was more eventful. For the Miami warriors followed him, striking detachments of his army at several points and killing a number of officers and men. The journey back to Fort Washington became a bedraggled retreat.

Through the snow Miami braves rode northward towards the Maumee, exultant at the success of their tactics against General Harmar. It was winter and their stores were low, but there were provisions coming

[190]

TWO GENERALS LOSE THEIR ARMIES

from the King's stores at Detroit and they had let enough blood to make them feel victorious.

December came and the tribes went into council, the purpose of which was the formation of a confederacy. Simon Girty spoke as one of the chiefs, saying: Let the white man go back across the Ohio and leave the Indian to his hunting ground. Let him break up the forts he has built on the north bank, else we will burn them for him. And let us assembled here send out the red belts of war to the chieftains of all the Indian tribes so that they may join us in driving the white man back where he came from! Blue Jacket, Tarhe, Little Turtle, Bockongahelas—all of the war chiefs spoke those words and were thereby heartened to believe that what they wanted would come to pass.

Not only did Simon urge the braves in the council house towards war, he was also ready, solely of his own accord, with a guiding hand in the field. Towards the end of the meeting he called to the warriors, asking them who would follow him down to the white man's forts.

Many answered his call. And while the war pole still shivered in the cold wind Girty led a pack down the long trail—it was nearly two hundred miles—to the neighborhood of Dunlap's Station, which then became his objective.

They left the Maumee in December, probably the

THE WHITE SAVAGE

middle of the month; for by January 8 a party of Girty's scouts who had followed down the Great Miami to within a few miles of the Dunlap settlement had come upon four white men. The frontiersmen were on the west bank, where they had camped the night before, had finished their breakfast and were unsuspectingly walking along the river when Girty's scouts fired at them from an ambush. One of the four men dropped dead; two wheeled and ran down the trail to the settlement, but the fourth was captured. His name was Abner Hunt, and the Indians, apparently satisfied that their job was done, bound him and carried him up the Great Miami towards Girty instead of pursuing the two that had escaped.

A day or so after the capture the braves and their prisoner met Girty coming down the river with his warriors, who were nearly three hundred in number. Hunt was terrified to stand before this darkly visaged white man in Indian dress. And from him Girty learned what there was to know about Dunlap's Station, that the settlement covered about an acre in which several cabins were enclosed by surrounding pickets; that at the corners of the pickets stood blockhouses in which the men could defend themselves from attack, and that of the men who were capable of bearing arms there were seventeen who belonged there regularly with their wives and children

TWO GENERALS LOSE THEIR ARMIES

and also eighteen private soldiers who had been sent there a short while before by General Harmar from Fort Washington. The whole was commanded by Lieutenant Jacob Kingsbury.

Taking Hunt with him, Girty and his three hundred braves moved on down the river and on the next night came quietly within sight of the stockade and prepared to make an overwhelming surprise in the morning. The braves were kept well within the surrounding woods and no fires showed through to the clearing. In a wide circle they lay on their arms and waited for dawn.

As the sun rose the savages appeared among the stumps in the fields about the stockade. They ran forward, howling and firing into the logs. But the two men who had escaped when Hunt was taken had hurried back to the stockade with the news that Indians were in the neighborhood and Lieutenant Kingsbury was somewhat prepared. The soldiers inside ran at once to the blockhouses and returned the fire through the loopholes, shooting so effectively that no Indian at any point got within reach of the pickets.

Now that the surprise attack had failed—for Girty's Indians could make no headway—a strange piece of strategy was employed. As his braves fell back among the trees some of them closed about Abner Hunt. And seeing him there the thought came into one of their

[193]

heads that through this prisoner they might be able to break down the morale of the garrison. A white flag was thrust into his hand and he was pushed forth through the clearing to within a stone's throw of the stockade. Girty told him, "Tell them to give up and we won't harm their lives or belongings; but if they don't, by God, we'll kill you; if they do we'll turn you loose."

The shot was stilled as Hunt appeared with the piece of white goods fluttering from the end of a stick which he held aloft. With two braves directly behind him and a host of others with their muskets leveled at him from the thicket in rear he was forced to mount a stump. There he began to deliver the hateful message which Girty had commanded of him. And having been promised his own liberty if he succeeded and his death if he failed, Hunt pleaded fervently, imploringly.

But inside the stockade there was little thought of opening the gates to a horde of war-heated savages who had traveled for nearly two weeks through the cold for the purpose of killing. Too many times in the past had white men listened to promises of that kind and had seen horrible consequences. Besides, though Kingsbury was nearly ten times outnumbered, the men were resolute enough not to give up hope. Only one man had been wounded in the first attack and, moreover, Fort Washington was not so far away but that troops could march from it to the aid of Dunlap's Station.

After Hunt's entreaties had sounded for some time he was brought down from the stump and the stick with the white flag broken. The firing recommenced.

The sun made its slow rise and descent to the accompaniment of whizzing musket balls and flying arrows. And when night came the thirty-five soldiers inside the stockade were still holding the warriors away from the pickets.

Some hours after dark two of Kingsbury's men left the station and after slipping unobserved through the Indian fires ran over the trail towards Fort Washington. Their departure made no interruption in the fight. Bullets spattered intermittently through the chill blackness that lay over the clearing and now and again a flaming arrow was launched upon the roof of a cabin or blockhouse.

Still the thirty-three men held out. Thinking to frighten them out of their fortitude the maddened savages, whether with or without Girty's sanction, determined to exhibit their powers on the luckless Hunt. Taking hold of him, they drew him into the clearing. There, in the remembrance of one of the men in the stockade, they tied him to a log, stretched him out and built a scorching fire around him. As he burned he screamed, but their own yells as they danced in a circle about him kept his voice from being heard. After a while the dancing and shouting ceased. Then Hunt's painful cries rose penetratingly. It was nearly dawn when he was silenced; he was dead.

The burning of Hunt was about the last act of Girty's party before Dunlap's Station. Before the day had brightened they had turned disappointedly towards the north again. Fortunate for them that they did, for hunters had brought word of the siege to Fort Washington and the two messengers who had escaped from the stockade that night met a body of troops the next morning only a few miles away.

Girty went back with them to the Maumee Rapids, but left soon afterward for his farm near Malden. Catharine, he knew, was going to produce another child and whether he went on that account or not he was there when the daughter was born and christened Sarah.

He remained throughout the winter and into the early spring on his farm. But when the thaw came he engaged a Canadian farmer to look after his fields and returned to the Maumee, where the British were building a fort at the foot of the Rapids.

During the spring and the following summer Simon heard the news from the banks of the Ohio. Down at

TWO GENERALS LOSE THEIR ARMIES

Fort Washington General St. Clair, as governor of the Northwest Territory, was sending out troops on short expeditions and being criticized for not taking the field with a greater force. Immigration was being held up by fear of the Indians and the men who had invested in and laid out the great tracts of land were not making money from their venture. People generally were of the opinion that the Indians ought to be driven so far up into the Ohio country that they would be unable to strike at the pioneers.

But Arthur St. Clair was hardly a war-like soul. Social amenities and a well-filled table were more appealing to his nature than a long journey through forests and swamps, with creeks and rivers that had to be forded or bridged. Also he was a victim of that prime eighteenth century complaint, the gout. However, something had to be done, and he, being governor of the territory and commander of the army there, had to do it.

From April until September was spent in concentrating troops and supplies at Fort Washington. By that time he had got an army of about twenty-three hundred, not counting the militia. He had also got between fifty and two hundred and fifty women who were to provide entertainment for the soldiers on the way. They would, of course, slow up the movements of his troops and he was greatly imperiling their lives by allowing them to go, but if it would make the soldiers and officers any happier to have wives and strumpets along —which it apparently would—he was willing that they should go.

In September he moved from Fort Washington to Fort Ludlow, which was six miles upward. And from there he advanced along the Great Miami to the location on which he built Fort Hamilton. Major General Richard Butler, between whom and himself there was a good deal of jealousy, was also along. Forty-four miles north of Hamilton he and Butler constructed another fort, which St. Clair called Fort Jefferson. With all of this protection behind him, with the camp women buzzing and gossiping about and with some soldiers who had rather not have gone, he set out to engage the Indians in the wilderness.

It was not long after General St. Clair began cutting his way up into the Indian country that the warriors gathered about the lower Maumee heard of his movements. Tecumseh, whose name in the Shawanese tongue signifies a shooting star, went down swiftly with a small group of braves and was soon shadowing the advance guard of the governor's unsuspecting army. And shortly St. Clair's line of march and the approximate number of his men were known at the Miami headquarters.

TWO GENERALS LOSE THEIR ARMIES

But this time the Indians did not fall back. All along the Maumee the tribes were daubing themselves with war paint and singing old songs of vengeance. Blue Jacket, who was tall and straight, rather dazzling in his crimson coat and red sash, struck the pole for the fierce Shawanese; Little Turtle, lighter skinned and more contemplative than his fellow leader, called to the Miami warriors; Captain Pipe was ready with a force of Delawares, and Simon Girty, looking like a musical comedy bandit in his bright silk handkerchief fitted over his dark, scarred poll and a brace of silver mounted pistols at his sides, prepared to ride at the head of the Wyandots.

Altogether there were less than fifteen hundred men who rode down to meet St. Clair's army. But they went quietly and easily, unhampered by the burdens of provisions, artillery and equipment that weighed down the Americans and required them to cut roads for passage wherever they went.

That was the first advantage possessed by the Indians. Another perhaps equally strong was that St. Clair, except on one occasion, had no scouting parties in front of his main body. There were also the troublesome women, at least one of whom carried a nursing child at her breast. And, to add to St. Clair's handicaps, not all of his men were willing to fight, for at least two hundred of them had deserted some days before they struck the Indian country.

This curious assemblage of white people which had come to drive four tribes out of the Ohio country was itself attacked as it lay encamped on the night of November third at a bend of the Wabash River in what became Mercer County, Ohio. St. Clair was surprised. The only warning he had came from the sounds of firing from some volunteer scouting parties which had gone out during the night and had a slight brush with an advance party of Indians.

A little after daybreak on November fourth the full attack began. The militia, encamped about a quarter of a mile in front of the main army, took the first blow and promptly fell back over the snow-covered ground and across the creek. Doubtless St. Clair heard them, but he did not see them, for at that time he was lying stretched out in his tent with a sudden and mortifying renewal of the gout.

The Indians came howling forward under a shower of shot and arrows. The Wyandots were leading and Girty was well to the fore. On the heels of the militia they came riding down through the woods and splashed over the river into the midst of the regulars. Some parts of the American line held, as men, not as military units. Major Jacob Fowler, who was at the battle as a second lieutenant, described the confusion for Cist's (Cincinnati) Advertiser: "One of Captain Piatt's men lay . . . shot through the belly. I saw an Indian behind a small tree, not twenty steps off, just outside the regular lines. He was loading his piece, squatting down as much as possible to screen himself. I drew sight at his butt and shot him through . . ." Then Colonel Darke came up through the mêlée, leading his men at the charge. "The Indians were driven by this movement clear out of sight, and the Colonel called a halt and rallied his men, who were about 300 in number. As an experienced woodsman and hunter [he was also, he modestly admits, a mere subaltern; but those were democratic days], I claimed the privilege of suggesting to the Colonel that where we then stood—there being a pile of trees blown out of root—would form an excellent breastwork, being of length sufficient to protect the whole force, and that we might yet need it; I judged by the shouting and firing that the Indians had closed up the gap we had made in charging, and told the colonel so." But though Fowler suggested a charge and the colonel told him to lead the way, the "Indians were so thick we could do nothing with them."

It was the flying Wyandots led by Girty that were so thick. They pushed through the soldiers' ranks, scattering destruction and driving them towards the baggage trains and the artillery, which were well into the camp. By the time the Wyandots had captured the rolling stock only ten per cent of Colonel Darke's men were left standing. But Fowler was still at hand: "I had been partially sheltered by a small tree, but a couple of Indians, who had taken a larger one, both fired at me at once, and feeling the steam of their guns at my belly, I supposed myself cut to pieces. But no harm had been done, and I brought my piece to my side and fired, without aiming at the man who stood his ground, the fellow being so close to me I could hardly miss him. I shot him through the hips and while he was crawling away on all fours Colonel Darke, who had dismounted and stood close by me, made at him with his sword and struck his head off . . ."

A little later there was a cry from the neighborhood of the tents. General St. Clair, who had hobbled from his bed and was trying to mount a horse which his orderlies were holding for him, was calling for the troops to charge the road. His adjutant general echoed the command.

But the order from St. Clair was not for an attack but for a break to safety. Already men and women were streaming down the freshly cut road and horses were plunging madly at the whoops and musketry of the onrushing Indians. St. Clair missed the stirrup of the

TWO GENERALS LOSE THEIR ARMIES

mare he was trying to mount. It ran off and another, a packhorse, was led up. On its broad back he ambled slowly away from the action.

Fowler, however, ran over to his relative, Captain Piatt, and "told him that the army was broken up and in full retreat."

"Don't say so," he replied, "you will discourage my men and I can't believe it."

Soon, however, Captain Piatt was convinced. "The bodies of the dead and dying were around us [Major General Butler's was one, but he was carried into a tent where a surgeon attended to his wounds] and the freshly scalped heads were reeking with smoke, and in the heavy morning frost looked like so many pumpkins through a cornfield in December."

By noon the Indians completely had the field and went to work with their scalping knives. For the retreating army had made no attempt to take care of the wounded. General Butler was one who had been left behind. He had lain outstretched with a bullet wound while the screaming Indians cut in among the deserted tents of the officers, the trains of baggage and ammunition which St. Clair's army had hastily abandoned. Helplessly he waited for someone to come.

Presently Girty and a Wyandot warrior detached themselves from the looting and scalping mêlée and rode up to the general's tent. Girty looked at Butler, whom he did not know but whose uniform showed him to be of high command, then turned to his Indian companion and observed, "Big, very big Long Knife captain." The warrior's tomahawk went up and down; General Butler was dead and ready to be hacked to pieces.

From all over the field where St. Clair's camp had been, came the thud of the tomahawk and the rip of the scalping knife. Horses plunged about without riders while braves reached out for their bridles; bewildered cattle ran with swinging heads; flour, ball and powder, clothing and blankets lay scattered everywhere.

Down along St. Clair's trace a few braves followed the retreating army for a dozen or more miles. And one woman, made frantic by the pursuit, flung the child that she was carrying into a snow pile, then ran the more swiftly back over the slushy trace towards distant Fort Washington.

When the looting and murder was finally over a deputation of Wyandots, who had been the leaders of the day, came respectfully up to Simon Girty and made a long speech in which they presented him with three of the captured cannon . . .

Simon Drives a Quill Through His Nostrils

CHAPTER X

Simon Drives a Quill Through His Nostrils

MANY of the Indians were brave, but not all of them were foolish. And after they had seen two expeditions of Americans drive towards the Miami towns they knew enough to withdraw to a locality that was less in the minds of the officers who commanded the forts down along the Ohio. Accordingly the Miamis and others who had been living about Kekiong-gay began to move eastward along the Maumee towards its junction with the Auglaize.

Scenically and productively that territory where the Indians now were intermingling was a delight. Most of the land was thickly wooded with walnut, oak, sycamore, maple and hickory; the two rivers meandered through soft ground and made a long, clear sweep of bottomland on either shore. Each spring the life of the soil was renewed by the floodwater, which deposited rich mud that made it excellent for cereals and vegetables; game was abundant; the fish were of various kinds and ran to prodigious sizes.

Here during that spring were gathered a thousand

or more Indians; they worked at building huts from logs blown down by the winds and covered them with bark and hides. They planted gardens and great fields, until by summer the banks of the Auglaize for some miles and those of the Maumee for even farther were lined with a tall stand of yellowing corn (the ears of which, as it happened, General Anthony Wayne, appointed by President Washington to take charge of operations in the Northwest, was inordinately fond of).

At that time, as for nearly a hundred years before, a number of white people were living with the Indians. Some of them were traders and had cabins on the highbanked point of land that lay between the Auglaize coming from the northwest and the Maumee from the southwest. One or two were British emissaries. The rest had been captured on raids upon the American settlement and were now adopted into the families which had taken them.

Of these white captives living about the Maumee at that time at least three have left some record of the manners and habits of Simon Girty. One of them, young Jonathan Alder, rather liked the pugnacious renegade and rather thought that reports of his cruelties had been exaggerated. Several times he had known Girty to effect the release of white prisoners, more than once at his own expense. He also thought that Simon had not shown the fiendishness of which he had been accredited at the burning of Colonel Crawford.

But Oliver Spencer, on the other hand, felt that Girty was the very substance of dangerous and malignant savagery. As a boy Oliver had been captured by the Shawanese in a raid on the settlement of Columbia, a few miles above Fort Washington, that summer. He was eleven years old at the time and after being brought to the new Maumee encampment he was placed in the family of an ancient squaw named Cooh-coo-cheeh and had for his adopted brother and sister, "a dark Indian girl (an orphan) two years my elder, and a half Indian boy, about a year younger than myself, both her grandchildren by her only daughter, now the wife of George Ironside, a British Indian trader living at the trading station on the high point directly opposite to her cabin a few hundred yards above the mouth of the Auglaize. [George Ironside, by the way, had an M. A. from King's College, Aberdeen.] The boy, reputed to be the son of the famous, or, rather, infamous renegade Simon Girty, was very sprightly, but withal, passionate and wilful, a perfectly spoiled child, to whom his mother had given the Mohawk name of Ked-zaw-saw, while his grandmother called him Simo-ne."

One day young Spencer was taken by his foster grandmother up the Auglaize to the Shawanese village of Blue Jacket. This war chief stood about six feet tall—"was finely proportioned, stout and muscular; his eyes large, bright and piercing; his forehead high and broad; his nose aquiline; his mouth rather wide, and his countenance open and intelligent, expressive of firmness and decision." The chieftain was gaudily clad in honor of another visitor who was soon to come—Simon Girty. Blue Jacket wore a scarlet tunic with gold lace and gold epaulets, a red sash around his waist and red moccasins and leggings. He was agreeable to young Spencer and allowed him to go inside the cabin. It was richly furnished with skins and adorned with war clubs, bows and beaded quivers, muskets, swords and tomahawks.

While young Spencer was there Girty arrived, but "whether it was from prejudice, associating with his look the fact that he was a renegade, the murderer of his own countrymen, racking his diabolical inventions to inflict new and more excruciating forms of torture, or not; his dark, shaggy hair, his low forehead; his brows contracted and meeting above the short, flat nose; his gray, sunken eyes, averting the ingenuous gaze; his lips thin and compressed, and the dark and sinister expression of his countenance, seemed to me the very picture of a villain. He wore the Indian costume, but without any ornament; and his silk handkerchief, while it supplied the place of a hat, hid an unsightly wound in his fore-

SIMON DRIVES A QUILL

head. On each side, in his belt, was stuck a silver mounted pistol, and at his left hung a short broad dirk, serving occasionally the uses of a knife."

On meeting the youth Girty straightened his shoulders and began asking countless questions. He wanted to know about Spencer's family and how he liked his captivity, yet he was more interested in the strength of the different garrisons on the Ohio, the number of American troops at Fort Washington and when President Washington planned to send another army against the Indians.

With old Cooh-coo-cheeh, Blue Jacket, and young Spencer standing there, Simon grew eloquent and vainglorious. "He spoke of the wrongs he had received at the hands of his countrymen, and with fiendish exultation, of the revenge he had taken. He boasted of his exploits, of the number of his victories, and of his personal prowess; then, raising his handkerchief and exhibiting the deep wound in his forehead (which I was afterwards told was inflicted by the tomahawk [sword] of the celebrated Indian chief, Captain Brant, in a drunken frolic) said it was a saber cut which he had received in battle at St. Clair's defeat, adding with an oath that he had 'sent the damned Yankee officer' that gave it 'to Hell.' He ended by telling me that I would never see home, but if I should 'turn out to be a good hunter and a brave warrior I might some day be a chief.'"

Young Spencer was frightened by the meeting and glad when old Cooh-coo-cheeh took him back to the cabin.

Another white captive on the Maumee at that time, however, owed his life to Simon Girty. His name was William May. After the Indians had brought him to their camp they had condemned him to death, had blackened his face, and were preparing the faggots about the stake. The laconic words of his own statement are "was condemned to die, but saved by Simon Girty."

May had been with the Indians at St. Clair's rout where Simon had fought with so much zeal. Which was not unusual, for in most of the larger engagements at that time there were white men—though they were given their choice and not required to take up arms—fighting with the Indians for the loot that would fall to the victor.

But in the smaller attacks, in the marauds, the white men were not allowed to take part. None, that is, except Simon Girty, who by this time was a renowned and trusted warrior among the Indians.

In the early summer when Spencer met him Simon raised a force of braves from the Maumee and journeyed at their head down to the south among the forts which

SIMON DRIVES A QUILL

the settlers were always building. It was June and the planting had been done; willingly a hundred braves followed him through the leafy forest to Fort Jefferson, where, concealing themselves in the surrounding wood, they watched sharply for the moment to attack.

Now Fort Jefferson had at that time, if Howe quoted aright, a very gullible commander, a Captain Shaylor, who was extraordinarily fond of hunting. And this penchant of his, it appears, was known to some of the Indians who surrounded the fort that summer. "Before they were discovered . . . [they] secreted themselves in some underbrush and behind some bogs near the fort . . . [where] they imitated the noise of turkeys. The captain, not dreaming of a decoy, hastened out with his son, Billy, expecting to return loaded with game. As they approached near the place the savages rose, fired, and his son, a promising lad, fell. The captain turning, fled to the garrison. The Indians pursued closely, calculating either to take him prisoner or enter the sally-gate with him in case it opened for his admission. They were, however, disappointed, though at his heels; he entered and the gate was closed the instant he reached it. In his retreat he was badly wounded by an arrow in his back."

Whether these extraordinarily wily braves were of Girty's party is nowhere stated, but it was within a few weeks of that time at most that the white leader appeared (June 25, 1792) before Fort Jefferson and waited until a number of the garrison went out to work in the cornfields. Then his braves leaped upon them and disposed of sixteen, either killed or taken prisoner. They left four bodies in the field behind them when they took the northward trail again.

From this raid Simon returned to the Maumee, where the chieftains were beginning to talk of holding another great council, perhaps the greatest of any ever held in the Ohio country. Girty was restless at this time, boastful, eager for any action that was directed against the Americans. He was glad when word was sent by runners with belts of wampum to the northwest tribes, the "seven nations of Canada, and of twenty-seven nations beyond Canada, as well as to the Gora tribe and to the Seneca-Iroquois. And the result was to be, if the Ohio Indians got what they wanted, a united front of all the tribes against the settlers. And what a marvelous battle might have followed! Thousands and thousands of Indians standing ready along the Maumee to await Wayne's army which was slowly coming. . . . However:

Weeks went by after the runners had gone out. The leaves began to turn the colors of autumn. And Girty, waiting for the council, again bethought himself of the

SIMON DRIVES A QUILL

American forts that lay southward. Organizing a party of some two hundred and fifty braves he struck down towards the Ohio again, his object being the capture of a supply train that was, he had heard, moving up to Fort Jefferson.

But his marauding party had not gone far when he was overtaken by a runner from the Maumee who brought word that the sachems were arriving from the other tribes and that he should be on hand for the deliberations. He turned back, gladly perhaps, for the meeting was of prime importance; he hoped that it would result in what at last amounted to a declaration of war by all the tribes, and he could not help feeling honored to be the only white man who would sit in the council. It was time to fight again.

When he arrived he found a vast gathering of important chiefs and sachems. Red Jacket—whose counsel against a general war was to delay the issue fatally—and forty-six other representatives of the Seneca-Iroquois, three chiefs of the Gora tribe, many from the far northwest; and besides these were present the heads of the Shawanese, the Delawares, Miamis, Wyandots, Pottawatomies and such offshoots from parent tribes as the Mingoes and Monseys.

They went into session in October in the grove on the high ground between the Maumee and Auglaize rivers. Simon was the only alien to sit with them in that stretch of mainland between the two streams. In a great clearing surrounded by tremendously branching trees, they kindled their council fires of the tied-up bundles of faggots brought from great distances and sat solemnly on their blankets while everybody listened to everybody else on the question of what should be done about these persistent and war-like white men, so much more war-like than themselves.

That anything could be done about it was a preposterous hope from the beginning. That all of the tribes, on such short notice, should overcome their various personal interests and unite! Perhaps it would never have been undertaken had it not been urged upon the Indians by men working through the British Indian Department, Sir John Johnson, Alexander McKee (who now had a post down at the foot of the rapids by the British fort), Simon Girty and others. As for the meeting itself it was broken up after a long harangue by Red Jacket, sachem of the Senecas, who pleaded with the Ohio Indians to withhold the declaration of war until the following spring, meanwhile giving the Americans a chance to meet them in a treaty. This was agreed to and a message was despatched to the United States Congress.

The long winter passed. Finally the answer came.

SIMON DRIVES A QUILL

Benjamin Lincoln, of Massachusetts, Beverly Randolph of Virginia and Timothy Pickering of Pennsylvania, all as United States commissioners, took ship northwesterly across Lake Erie to the mouth of the Detroit River, where they prepared to deal with the Ohio tribes. They stayed at the house of Matthew Elliott, which was some distance south of the Girty farm at Malden. From here the commissioners apprised the Indians of their readiness to treat.

So at last the commissioners had come! Down along the Maumee Indian chiefs were chosen to meet them. They went in boats and Girty, Elliott and Alexander McKee accompanied them. It was on an island from which could be seen Elliott's house that the representatives of the Indians met the representatives of the United States. There were no handclasps, no greetings or signs of mutual esteem.

Girty's voice rolled forth insolently. Were these commissioners, he wanted to know in the name of the Ohio Indians, ready and authorized to fix the Ohio River as the south and west boundary of the native's territory? And as he made this astounding remark he "supported," it is said, "his insolence" with a quill driven through his nose beneath the nostrils.

The commissioners stepped grimly back and replied flatly that they were not so authorized. What they had come for was to get more land, not to relinquish what they had already claimed.

Very well then; there was no use of further talk, said Girty, interpreting. The chiefs and their white allies turned their backs.

But another voice, an Indian's, arose. There was use in talking; the sachems would have to consult their families again; let the commissioners wait until they had done so.

The Indians and their white friends went away in their boats again. The commissioners remained, waiting to hear from them, smiling at their ridiculous request for the Ohio River as the south and west boundary of their lands.

Weeks passed. It was summer. The commissioners had stayed near the mouth of the Detroit River. For they could afford to wait. General Wayne, who had been organizing the Legion of the United States when they left on their mission, was now at Fort Washington, where he was drilling his rough-neck volunteers into an obedient corps that was fit to fight Indians. Also John Jay was in London negotiating for a final treaty with England which would drive the British out of the Ohio country when the agreement had finally been reached.

At last a message came from the council on the Maumee. It notified the commissioners that the only boundary to which the Indians could agree was the Ohio River. Very well again! Pickering, Lincoln and Randolph knew the United States would never consent to that. They went home.

The Long Shadow of Mad Anthony Wayne

CHAPTER XI

The Long Shadow of Mad Anthony Wayne

IT was August, 1793, when the commissioners departed. Throughout the fall, the winter, and the spring of 1794 the Indians remained stubborn and fiery and would accept no less than the Ohio River as the boundary between themselves and the frontiersmen. For Simon Girty it was a time of restless waiting. He and the war chiefs knew that General Wayne had come up farther into their country and was making ready to attack them. But the Indians then had no thought of defeat. Their success over St. Clair had given them immense confidence and rather than fearing Wayne's approach they were pleased that he was coming. For they coveted the horses, blankets, firearms and provisions that he would bring, and they had tall hopes of getting them. Their spies watched him advance towards the spot where St. Clair had been cut up; and twice their warriors charged into detachments of his army. The first time the braves rushed upon the cavalry and were quickly driven back, but on the next day about forty of them discovered a supply train guarded by an escort of ninety men; and charging into it, they killed a great number and rode off sixty-four horses.

From the time General Wayne got within a hundred miles of the Maumee the war chiefs were kept informed of the general movements of his army and of its approximate size, which was then about fifteen hundred. They knew when his line of march veered off from the Great Miami and drew him near to St. Clair's battlefield. They knew that he stopped about six miles above Fort Jefferson and there began to erect small cabins for winter quarters and to surround them with a huge stockade and a line of pickets. Their spies saw his men come still closer, to the very ground by the creek where the Indians had been so victorious and where the skulls of more than six hundred white men lay above the earth.

It was there that General Wayne built Fort Recovery, which was an advance post for his main garrison, Fort Greenville. The Indians knew these things, which were of the sort that had helped them to defeat Colonel Crawford, to harry and confuse Harmar, and to destroy St. Clair. But this time their knowledge was of little use to them. Though every night runners and spies reported Wayne's movements, they also brought the news that he was always on the alert. They said that "when he was on the march, that it was next to impossible to get a horse out of his camp" and "that at night Wayne would

Brigadier General Anthony Wayne

cut down great trees, and fence in a tract of land large enough to hold his entire army and baggage, and that these fences were built so high that none could get at them, and but few could get out." And after Fort Greenville went up Wayne was even more inaccessible.

The winter passed. At Wayne's headquarters his army marked time. Up on the Maumee Simon Girty went about among his friends, talking to Blue Jacket, to Captain Pipe, to Tarhe the Crane, to Little Turtle and to Captain Brant. Let the Indians continue in their purpose to fight; let them stand ready to attack, to come down with the force and unexpectedness of the cyclone upon this Big White Captain and his Long Knife warriors! The Big Captain would yet grow careless, the Indians would defeat him, and all of the Ohio country would be theirs! A man of temper, he was irritated by the long days of inactivity, the more so because he felt the menace of the Americans, who were establishing themselves ever nearer to him. They had had a reward posted for his scalp; there were the various threats which they had made; what would they, he wondered, do to him if they caught him? It wasn't very pleasant to think about.

But he stayed on. Whether it was that he had hope of the Indians again defeating United States soldiers, that he felt himself bound to remain with them, that he was simply carrying out his job, or that he was impelled to defy his former countrymen to the last—whatever the reason, he remained on the Maumee throughout the spring and early summer.

An opening for an attack came in June and Simon was ready to take part in it. Indian scouts in the neighborhood of Wayne's main army (where Mad Anthony, still at Fort Greenville, was awaiting reinforcements from Kentucky that would nearly double the size of his command) reported to their chieftains that the party of Long Knives that held Fort Recovery were growing less cautious; from time to time American convoys traveled between Recovery and Greenville; moreover, the former stronghold did not seem to be impregnable.

It was the kind of news that Girty, Blue Jacket, and the rest were waiting for. They called to the braves, who needed no persuading. Eager for revenge and inspired by the thought of the heavy supply trains that had traveled with Wayne's army, more than a thousand of them set out to attack Fort Recovery and to retrieve, if possible, the cannons which had been presented to Girty but which he had failed to take with him from St. Clair's battleground.

On the morning of June 30, they had come to the edge of a forest within a few miles of the fort. They were riding cautiously forward into the tall grass when of a sudden there was a cry of, "Indians! Indians!" and they were discovered by a body of ninety riflemen and fifty cavalrymen. These men were under the command of Major McMahon. The Indians rushed forward with a whoop.

McMahon's outfit, most of whom were afoot, wheeled and ran before that thundering, howling mob of savage horsemen. Even the soldiers that were mounted were put in such a fear that they slid off their saddles and rushed for the gates. Inside the pickets the alarm was given and shot began to pour out from loopholes in the walls and blockhouses. Well-saddled horses, bereft of their riders, galloped confusedly about, jerking their heads up to avoid the outstretched hands of Indians.

Under the commands of Blue Jacket, who was assisted by Little Turtle and Girty, the braves strung out around the fort, encircling it completely and firing from behind trees and fallen logs. But the bullets continued to spit out at them from the pickets. Up into the air and down whirred the shell from a mortar. It dropped with a great burst and a black cloud of pungent smoke. The mortar, the marksmanship of the men behind the barricade, were disconcerting, but the Indians kept on crawling forward in small parties, trying to reach the walls. Some of them got within fifty yards of the fort.

THE WHITE SAVAGE

There they ran, half bent over, their attention divided between overthrowing the defense and capturing the frightened horses which reared among the stumps and saplings.

Throughout the day the siege continued, but as darkness fell there was a lull. No considerable number had fallen on either side. But Blue Jacket had discovered that his tactics were unavailing. He drew his force a mile down the creek and determined to wait until a little before dawn when he would make a surprise attack.

Before sunrise the surprise assault was tried. But that too was a failure. Musketry crackled for an hour or more; by daylight there were more than fifty casualties inside the fort, but a much greater number among the Indians. During the early hours of the first of July there was little firing from the savages. They had come to feel that the fort could not be taken. And after rescuing their wounded, some of whom had to be carried in broad light from the very shadows of the pickets, and capturing about two hundred and fifty horses, they made the long retreat back to the Maumee.

Girty was reluctant to abandon the attack and gloomy on the return ride. To lose on the exact ground where St. Clair's army had been cut up was a bad omen. He knew, also, that Wayne's main body had not even been touched, that the Indian force of about twelve hundred

THE SHADOW OF ANTHONY WAYNE

had been repelled by merely an advance post of greatly inferior numbers. But his stubborn fury, his fear of the Americans, and perhaps his friendship for the Indians still governed his actions, making him remain in the dangerous Ohio country when it was no longer necessary for him to be there. It was not that he hadn't other places to go, for he had: his home was waiting for him, a fairly well developed farm, a house that for those days was comfortable, and a growing family. He could have gone to Malden and stayed there, retiring on half pay. But he chose to hire a man to work his land while he himself urged the Indians to stand fast on the Maumee and meet Wayne in battle.

For the Indians were in need of support. Though Blue Jacket's stalwart six-foot frame and ineradicable hatred stood as encouragement towards victory, the defeat at Fort Recovery had lowered the warriors' spirits and many of them were willing to listen to Little Turtle —a brave man, an able commander, but a thoughtful man as well—who advised them to arrange a treaty with the oncoming Americans and thus save their families from a bloody war. His opinion then was the same as it was later when he spoke at the general council, when he told them on August 19, "We have beaten the enemy twice, under separate commanders. We cannot expect the same good fortune always to attend us. The Amer-

THE WHITE SAVAGE

icans are now led by a chief who never sleeps. The night and the day are alike to him. During all the time he has been marching on our villages, notwithstanding the watchfulness of our young men, we have been unable to surprise him. Think well of it. There is something whispers me it would be prudent to listen to his offers of peace."

Prudent, yes, but whether the Indians fought or parleyed the result would have been the same: for the Americans wanted their land and meant to have it. And General Wayne was determined to subjugate the Ohio tribes even though in so doing it might mean a war with England, which General Washington had especially instructed him against.

However, the majority of the warriors had less faith in treaties than in arms. They were being well supplied with guns and ammunition by the British; at the foot of the Rapids stood Fort Miami, whose garrison under Major William Campbell, cannon and solid walls they expected to be defended by; also there were about three thousand braves who had come together between the Grand Glaize and the British fort. Therefore it was the words of Girty and Blue Jacket that they applauded.

In July, a few weeks after the attack on Fort Recovery, Wayne got his reinforcements. Major General Charles Scott, with sixteen hundred Kentucky volunteers, had arrived at Fort Greenville on July 26 and two days later Mad Anthony gave orders for the advance.

The Legion went slowly and cautiously, preceded by a number of scouts familiar with the country. The weather was hot and most of the water stagnant; from Fort Recovery onward roads had to be cut through the wilderness and bridges built over the swamps. Wayne found the mosquitoes "very troublesome and larger than I ever saw," was compelled to dig holes in the marshes in order that his troops might have water, dragged his heavy carriages through this strange land at the galling rate of about ten miles a day, incautiously got in the way of a falling tree and was nearly killed, yearned for salt, green corn and more rum.

But finally he came out upon what was called the Grand Glaize, the junction of the Maumee and Auglaize rivers. He thought the country thereabouts the most beautiful of any in the west "and believed equal by none in the Atlantic states. Here are vegetables of every kind in abundance, and we have marched four or five miles in cornfields down the Oglaize and there is not less than one thousand of acres of corn around the town." (There was to be scarcely any standing when he left.)

The Indians, of course, had deserted their towns. The day before, the last of the inhabitants had left, having been warned by a runner who came rushing through the fields and whooping the alarm. At once the remaining Indians gathered up all they could carry and took the trail down the Maumee towards the foot of the Rapids where warriors of half a dozen tribes were hesitantly making ready for battle.

For the Indians were not to be caught by any army that called fifteen miles a good day's march and who gave away their approach by smoke, fire and gunshot. They knew better tactics for enemy country than that. Yet despite all this it was the Indians who eventually were surprised.

At Camp "Grand Oglaize" [so he spelled Auglaize] General Wayne, expecting an attack and wanting to secure his position there in what had become the heart of the Indian country, built Fort Defiance. During the eight days which passed before it was finished he sent a messenger down the river to the Rapids, from where the Indians were watching him. The messenger carried the word that the Big White Captain considered the Indians to be his brothers, that Simon Girty, McKee, Elliott, and the rest from Detroit had neither the power nor the inclination to protect them and that they should at once send deputies to meet him halfway between his camp and Fort Miami, the British stronghold, "in order to settle the preliminaries of a lasting peace."

THE SHADOW OF ANTHONY WAYNE

This message was received and answered, but not, it seems likely, by a general council of the warriors. The reply given Wayne was a request for time, ten days in which the Indians agreed to make up their minds as to whether they would fight or parley; but if this extension were not granted them, they added, they would give battle when Wayne moved upon them.

Wayne was already on the march when this answer arrived. And that night he recorded in his journal the bare fact of the Indians' counter-proposal and made no mention of how he considered it. The next day, however, the army went on as before and encamped that night at the head of the rapids, one day's march from the British fort and the assembled Indians.

On the following night, that of August 19, the warriors held their final council; and it was then that Little Turtle made his plea for a peaceful meeting with the Big White Captain. The warriors listened, but in a frowning silence. And when Little Turtle had finished one of them offered the opinion that the reason Chief Little Turtle talked like that was because he felt fear.

There was no more to be done. Even as the warriors sat in a circle before their fires that night General Wayne was writing that in the morning his men would be ready for action, "providing the enemy have the presumption to favor us with an interview, which if they should think proper to do, the troops are in such high spirits that we will make an easy victory of them." As he wrote, Wayne could hear his pioneer companies throwing up shovelfuls of dirt, and felling logs to make a lightwork that would secure the baggage. For he knew he was within striking distance of the Indians and he wanted his men to be walking lightly when he struck them. But where the warriors sat the only sounds besides their voices came from the low water streaming brokenly down over the rock-bedded river.

After the unsatisfactory break-up of the council, most of the braves and chieftains spread their blankets and lay down to sleep, thinking that in the morning they would return again to the clutter of uprooted trees— the havoc of a cyclone some time past—where for three days they had lain in wait for Wayne's army. Having had no answer from him with regard to the ten days' armistice, they had been expecting him since the morning after the messenger had gone.

The stretch of fallen timber was along the north bank of the river a few miles up from the British fort and directly within Wayne's line of march. On the first morning the warriors had gone there—without breakfast, as was their custom when expecting to fight —and had waited throughout the day. Only at night had they gone back down the river to their kettles and blankets, and then they had been hungry. On the second day this was repeated. So that by the morning of the twentieth they had become disgusted with fasting till evening—furthermore, it was possible that Wayne intended to grant them the ten days. Something like that they must have thought, for they were woefully unprepared on the morning of the battle.

They were so poorly prepared that it was as if they had not expected combat that day at all. Of the (about) three thousand warriors in the neighborhood less than a third were near their positions in the fallen timber when the first shot was fired. The rest were lolling in the meadows near the British fort, talking and sitting around their steaming kettles. Captain Brant, in command of four hundred Mohawks who had come there to take part in the fight, was somewhere in the vicinity, but nobody seems to have discovered just where he was or what he was doing. Girty also was at hand, but not in the fort and not with the Indians. He did not emerge that day.

Wayne's army approached, the regulars, who were on the right, flanked by the river and covered in front, left flank and rear by Scott's mounted volunteers. As they came near the fallen timber the Indians on the ground opened fire and the advance guard "retreated in the utmost confusion," according to General Wayne.

THE WHITE SAVAGE

For a while it seemed as if the whole army would run. Captain Howell Lewis' outfit began to falter, turn and flee. But then there was a charge led around the right flank by Captain Campbell, who commanded the Legion cavalry. The men went swinging through the corn with muskets and sabers and the Indians scampered from their cover like so many rabbits.

Everywhere the Indians were running. At the fort they clamored at the doors, shouting and bewildered. But the doors remained closed and the guns of the British were silent. And by noon General Wayne was entering into a long argument with the commandant, and all the warriors that could walk had either disappeared or had been taken prisoner.

From somewhere in the vicinity of Fort Miami Simon Girty heard the news of the disaster and tried furiously to rally the Indians. But it was not to be done. Wayne had come upon them and was prepared to stay until they were broken. Fort Defiance gave him strong protection and he stayed there until about the middle of September, maintaining a strict watch for a counter-attack and meanwhile inviting the braves to attend the belated council.

It was the end. In England an agreement had been made through John Jay between Britain and America which tied the hands of the Indian service and required Canada to give up Detroit. And the Indians themselves, beaten and disorganized, were forced to follow General Wayne down to Fort Greenville where, in the following year, they agreed to limit their wanderings to a little corner in Northwestern Ohio.

Simon watched all this with an inflamed, befuddled eye. The British were giving up Detroit. He couldn't understand it. It didn't seem right. He was there on the day the last of them moved out in the face of the American troops who were coming to take command. He watched the people chuck great stones down into the wells, filling them up so that there would be no drinking water; smashing the windows of their erstwhile houses, locking the doors and throwing away the keys—but his expression of scorn and undying defiance had to be something greater than that, something picturesque and lasting. He sat on his horse near the edge of the high river bank, watching the American troops approaching from the south. Across the river was Malden and he could see his farm and cabin under a row of trees that fringed the opposite shore. Still he waited, and the Americans came closer.... Finally, with a shout and a curse, Simon dug the rowels into the mare's flanks and sent her forward. She leaped and there was a splash below. But as the waves smoothed out old

THE WHITE SAVAGE

Simon reappeared, still in the saddle and facing away from the country from which he was banned. After a while the mare clambered up on the Canadian shore and Simon headed her towards the cabin.

The Last Ride from the Tavern

CHAPTER XII

The Last Ride from the Tavern

*F*EW men, no matter what kind of lives they lead, survive their obituaries. But that was the fortune of Simon Girty. Whether it was because Americans in general refused to admit that a man could desert the United States, make war against it, and yet go unpunished (hence the fiction taught school children that Benedict Arnold died in poverty and disgrace), or whether it was taken for granted that all undesirables were killed at the battle of the Thames in the War of 1812, the following appeared in the Missouri Gazette for May 7, 1814, when Simon's life had four years still to run:

"Simon [Girty] was adopted by the Senecas, and became as expert a hunter as any of them. His character, as related in Kentucky and Ohio, 'of being a savage, merciless monster' is much exaggerated. It is true that he joined the Indians in most of their war parties, and conformed to their mode of warfare, but it is well authenticated that he saved many prisoners from death. He was considered an honest man, paying his debts to the last cent; and it is known that he sold his only horse

THE WHITE SAVAGE

to discharge a claim against him. It is true that he was a perfect Indian in his manners; that his utmost felicity was centered in a keg of rum; that under its influence he was abusive to all around him, even to his best friends. Yet we must recollect that his education was barbarous, and that mankind are more apt to sink into barbarism than they are to acquire the habits of civilized life.

"For the last ten years he had been crippled with rheumatism, yet he rode to his hunting grounds in pursuit of game, and would boast that he preserved a warlike spirit in the midst of bodily pain, and would often exclaim, 'May I breathe my last on the field of battle.' In this wish Simon was gratified; for in the battle of the Moravian towns, on the river Thames, he was cut to pieces by Colonel Johnson's mounted men. . . ."

When the foregoing (an extract from a sketch of the Girty brothers) was published, Simon was at the Mohawk village of Burlington Heights in Canada. Age and a too active life had left him stiff and gnarled, and when he walked it was to hobble about slowly and uncertainly. At this time he had already made his will, giving to his son Thomas his eighty-two acre farm in the first concession in the Malden township. He was definitely an old man; his hair had turned white and his skin was loose and leathery. And at Burlington Heights he was unhappy.

THE LAST RIDE

He had gone to Burlington Heights after the American victories about Lake Erie in the War of 1812, had gone to live with the Indians again so as to be far away from the Ohio and Kentucky soldiers who had reached the Canadian side of the Detroit River. But now it was different living among the braves and squaws. For in the old days he had his musket to depend on to supply his wants. But in these latter times the gun was shaky in his hands and he tired quickly riding after game. And sometimes he would look with quiet envy at the old men of the Mohawk family with whom he lived. For they had their sons and grandsons to provide for them and to listen to their sage counsel. But for Simon there was nobody.

Thomas, his best loved boy, had died, his heart failing from carrying a wounded British officer from the field. Simon would have to make a new will, or else let the property go whatever way it would. He wasn't sure about Catharine, his wife. It had been some years since she had shared his cabin, but that was his fault, not hers. In fact he had practically driven her out, whirling his sword blade around his head as he had done and cursing and threatening to lay the flat of it against her. He ought not to have done that, but somehow Catharine had got "right cantankerous" of late. She talked so much about religion and the after life—of which Simon cared nothing; and she told him it was sinful to drink as he did. At last she had gone and now he didn't know whether there was anybody in the cabin or not. . . . The Americans had burned many of the houses when they came to Malden; it would be luck if his own still stood.

His eyesight was failing. Though his return to Malden was not agreeable to contemplate, he knew he would have to go back. He knew he could not stay on with the Indians, for he had become a nuisance to them. Besides, he wanted to see the old farm again, to know how Ann and Peter Govereau, her husband, were getting along. So he saddled his mare and made the slow ride back to Malden.

Afterwards he was glad. For he found the cabin still unharmed and his son Prideaux living in it. He too must live there, Prideaux told him. And Peter Govereau kept a tavern at Amherstberg, which was just enough of a journey to give his old bones exercise. Then pretty soon Catharine came back; she came to cook and care for him and talk to him about religion.

But when he got weary of Catharine's voice there was always the tavern at Amherstberg. Peter and Ann were good to him and rather proud of him. His name by that time was familiar throughout all the west and middle west and when strangers came to Amherstberg

THE LAST RIDE

for a night's lodging Ann took delight in pointing out the white-haired, slumped and almost sightless figure sitting before his noggin of rum. She would ask, "Do you know who that is?" "No," the stranger would reply. And then Ann or Peter would answer respectfully, "Well, that's Simon Girty!" Whereupon the visitor would stare more intently and think, perhaps aloud, "He don't look so terrible; not for a man who had the name of being so great a villain."

For four years Simon lived amid these surroundings, which were now and again enlivened by the appearance of one of his Indian friends who had stopped in passing to talk to him. Or some old veteran would come down from Malden, where there was now a British fort, and sit, toothlessly garrulous.

But all the old people were dropping off. General Wayne, now, had been dead for more than twenty years. . . . And old Tarhe the Crane, they had just buried him on the Sandusky with the great to-do the Indians made when they paid the last honors to one of their chieftains. . . . And down in Kentucky at Locust Grove, George Rogers Clark, his heart gone wrong from too much whisky drunk to drown his poverty and the neglect of which he felt himself the victim, was ready to die. . . . And old Blue Jacket, they had buried him at an Ottawa village up the Auglaize. . . . As for Lit-

THE WHITE SAVAGE

tle Turtle, for five years he had been under the grass that grew about Kekiong-gay.

In the middle of February, 1818, Simon was attacked by illness one day as he returned to his cabin from the Amherstberg tavern. It was an extraordinarily bitter winter with tremendous drifts of snow. He had tired himself and had been chilled; when he got home he went to bed with a fever. That night he was no better and Catharine came and sat by his side.

The next day was worse and what was left of his rugged figure seemed to be shriveling up. His legs, as he would look down the quilt at them, appeared like two little hickory sticks, they were so thin and unreal to him. And Catharine began talking of religion and God and Jesus Christ. He lay with his face averted, his cheek against the pillow while he wondered helplessly, "why did women want to take on like that!"

He had been a sinner. He had killed a heap of folk. All the marauds he had led against the settlements, all the forts he had stormed, the pitched battles in which he had struck out so mightily. Could he be ashamed of them, crawl and grovel, ask repentance now that they were gone?

It snowed again the next day, and outside the cabin the wind drove ridges of white, deep, rolling drifts. The flakes became a blur to him, Catharine's voice grew

THE LAST RIDE

indistinct and distant, outside the door the creak of heavy boots tiptoeing was no longer heard. . . .

But two days later the planks of the cabin floor resounded. Despite the weather, the neighbors were coming from near and far. Catharine, Ann, Prideaux, Sarah, Peter, Joseph Munger stood white-faced and quiet while red-jacketed soldiers from Fort Malden marched through the heavy drifts and entered the door. By that time Simon was in a coffin, and down the road a detachment was digging into the frozen ground with picks and shovels.

Soldiers lifted him up and the procession filed slowly out. They walked towards the gate, but there the drifts were so high that the burden could not be carried through. After a moment a passage was found and Simon was lifted over the fence and down the road. A little later a salute of musketry roared into the biting air. As the smoke cleared away the soldiers marched northward, while the mourners moved back towards the cabin. Simon remained where he was, stationary at last.

Note

NOTE

The bulk of the foregoing material concerning the life of Simon Girty had already been gathered by Consul Willshire Butterfield, who published it in his "History of the Girtys"; Robert Clarke & Co., Cincinnati, 1890. Other works which have been read in connection with the writing of the present volume are: A Narrative of the Mission of the United Brethren Among the Delawares and Mohegan Indians, from its commencement in the year 1740, to the close of the Year 1808. By the Rev. John Heckewelder. Philadelphia, M'Carty and Davis, 1820; The Winning of the West. By Theodore Roosevelt. G. P. Putnam's Sons, New York, 1889-99; The Washington-Irvine Correspondence, arranged and annotated by C. W. Butterfield. Madison, Wisconsin, David Atwood, 1882. The Indian Captivity of O. M. Spencer, edited by Milo Milton Quaife (The Lakeside Classics), R. R. Donnelly & Sons, Chicago, 1917. The Magazine of American History. Transactions of the American Philosophical Society, Philadelphia, Abraham Small, 1819, Volume 1. An Account of the History, Manners and Customs of the Indian Natives who once inhabited Pennsylvania and Neighboring States, by the Rev. John Heckewelder, Howe's Historical Collections of Ohio. Columbus, 1900. A History of the Mississippi Valley, by John R. Spears and A. H. Clarke, A. S. Clarke, publisher, New York, 1903. American State Papers (Indian Affairs), Volume One, A History of Defiance (Ohio) County, Chicago, 1883. A Short Biography of John Leith, a reprint with illustrative notes by C. W. Butterfield, Robert Clarke & Co., Cincinnati, 1883. The History of Detroit and Michigan by Silas Farmer, Silas Farmer & Co., Detroit, 1884. Notes on the Settlement and Indian Wars of the Western Parts of Virginia and Pennsylvania from 1763 to 1783, etc., by Joseph Doddridge, Albany, New York, Joel Munsell, 1876. Sketches of Western Adventure, by John A. McClung, Ells, Claflin & Co., Dayton, O., 1847. Biographical Sketches, etc., by John McDonald, E. Morgan & Son, Cincinnati, 1838. Frontier Defense on the Upper Ohio—1777-78 (Draper Series Vol. III), edited by Reuben Gold Thwaites and Louise Phelps Kellogg, Wisconsin Historical Society, Madison, 1912. The Westward Movement, by Justin Winsor, Houghton, Mifflin, 1897. Articles on Americana from the American Historical Record.

www.ingramcontent.com/pod-product-compliance
Lightning Source LLC
Chambersburg PA
CBHW030319100526
44592CB00010B/490